Microsoft Forms

Complete Guide for Effective Surveys and Quizzes

Kiet Huynh

Table of Contents

CHAPTER I
Introduction to Microsoft Forms

1.1 What is Microsoft Forms?

Microsoft Forms is a versatile and powerful tool within the Microsoft 365 suite, designed to create surveys, quizzes, and polls with ease. Launched in 2016, it has quickly become a go-to solution for educators, businesses, and organizations looking to gather information efficiently. Microsoft Forms provides an intuitive interface that allows users to create, share, and analyze forms in real time, making it a valuable resource for data collection and analysis.

1.1.1 Overview of Microsoft Forms

Microsoft Forms is a cloud-based application that is part of the Microsoft 365 ecosystem. It enables users to create forms for various purposes, such as surveys, quizzes, and polls, which can be distributed to respondents via links, emails, or embedded on websites. The application offers a range of question types, including multiple choice, text, rating, date, and more, allowing users to tailor their forms to meet specific needs.

One of the standout features of Microsoft Forms is its user-friendly interface. Even individuals with little to no technical expertise can create professional-looking forms in minutes. The drag-and-drop functionality, coupled with pre-designed templates, simplifies the form creation process. Users can customize the appearance of their forms by selecting themes, adjusting colors, and adding images or videos, making their forms more engaging and visually appealing.

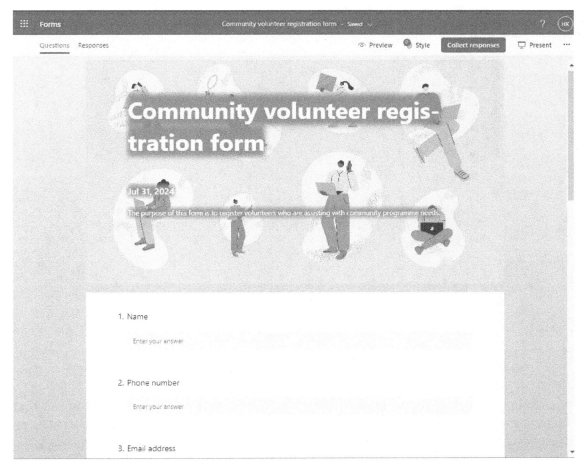

Another key aspect of Microsoft Forms is its integration with other Microsoft 365 applications. Forms can be seamlessly linked with Excel, SharePoint, Teams, and other Microsoft tools, enhancing their utility and providing additional avenues for data analysis and collaboration. For instance, responses from a form can be automatically exported to Excel for in-depth analysis or shared within a Teams channel for collaborative discussion.

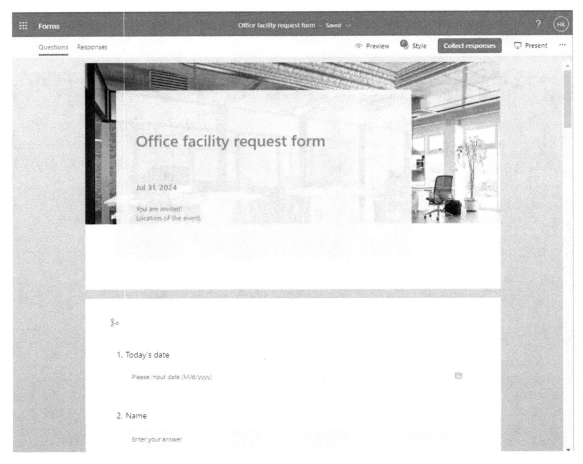

Microsoft Forms also supports branching logic, allowing creators to design forms that adapt based on respondents' answers. This feature enhances the user experience by presenting relevant follow-up questions, thereby reducing form fatigue and improving the accuracy of collected data.

In terms of data security, Microsoft Forms adheres to the stringent security standards set by Microsoft. Data is encrypted both in transit and at rest, ensuring that sensitive information is protected. Additionally, Microsoft Forms complies with major data protection regulations, such as GDPR, making it a trustworthy tool for organizations that prioritize data privacy.

1.1.2 Benefits of Using Microsoft Forms

Microsoft Forms is a versatile tool that offers a wide range of benefits for individuals and organizations alike. As a part of the Microsoft 365 suite, it seamlessly integrates with other Microsoft applications, enhancing productivity and collaboration. Here, we will explore the key benefits of using Microsoft Forms:

1. User-Friendly Interface

Microsoft Forms boasts an intuitive and user-friendly interface, making it accessible to users of all skill levels. Whether you are a beginner or an experienced user, the straightforward design allows you to create and manage forms effortlessly. The drag-and-drop functionality for adding questions and the easy customization options contribute to a smooth user experience. This simplicity encourages more people within an organization to adopt the tool, thereby increasing overall efficiency.

2. Versatility in Form Types

Microsoft Forms supports a variety of form types, including surveys, quizzes, and polls. This versatility allows users to gather different types of data for various purposes. For example, educators can use quizzes to assess student learning, while businesses can use surveys to collect customer feedback or conduct market research. The ability to create different types of forms within a single platform reduces the need for multiple tools and streamlines the data collection process.

3. Real-Time Collaboration

Collaboration is a critical component of many projects, and Microsoft Forms facilitates real-time collaboration among team members. Multiple users can work on a form simultaneously, making it easy to create, edit, and review forms as a group. This feature is particularly useful for distributed teams, enabling seamless collaboration regardless of geographical location. Additionally, the integration with Microsoft Teams further enhances collaborative efforts by allowing users to share forms and collect responses directly within the Teams environment.

4. Integration with Microsoft 365

One of the standout benefits of Microsoft Forms is its integration with other Microsoft 365 applications, such as Excel, SharePoint, and OneDrive. This integration allows for seamless data flow between applications, enhancing productivity and enabling comprehensive data analysis. For instance, responses collected through Microsoft Forms can be easily exported to Excel for advanced data analysis and visualization. This interoperability reduces the need for manual data transfer and minimizes the risk of errors.

5. Customization and Branding

Microsoft Forms offers extensive customization options, allowing users to tailor forms to meet specific needs and preferences. Users can choose from a variety of themes, colors, and fonts to match their organization's branding or the purpose of the form. Additionally, the ability to add images and videos to forms enhances engagement and makes the forms more visually appealing. Customization not only improves the user experience but also ensures that forms are consistent with the organization's branding guidelines.

6. Accessibility Features

Microsoft Forms is designed with accessibility in mind, ensuring that everyone, including individuals with disabilities, can use the tool effectively. Features such as screen reader support, keyboard navigation, and high contrast modes make it easier for users with visual or motor impairments to interact with forms. By prioritizing accessibility, Microsoft Forms ensures that organizations can reach a wider audience and comply with accessibility standards.

7. Data Security and Privacy

Data security and privacy are paramount considerations for any organization. Microsoft Forms adheres to robust security protocols to protect user data. Data collected through forms is stored securely within the Microsoft 365 environment, which is compliant with various industry standards and regulations, including GDPR. Additionally, users have control over who can access their forms and responses, allowing them to set permissions and protect sensitive information. These security features provide peace of mind and ensure that data is handled responsibly.

8. Analytics and Reporting

Analyzing the data collected through forms is crucial for deriving insights and making informed decisions. Microsoft Forms provides built-in analytics and reporting features that allow users to view response summaries and individual responses in real-time. The visual representation of data through charts and graphs makes it easier to interpret results and identify trends. Furthermore, the ability to export data to Excel enables more advanced analysis and reporting, supporting data-driven decision-making processes.

9. Automated Workflows

The integration of Microsoft Forms with Microsoft Power Automate (formerly known as Microsoft Flow) enables users to create automated workflows based on form responses. This automation can significantly enhance efficiency by automating repetitive tasks and streamlining processes. For example, a workflow can be set up to send an email notification whenever a new response is received or to update a SharePoint list with the form data. Automation reduces manual intervention, minimizes errors, and frees up time for more strategic activities.

10. Scalability

Microsoft Forms is scalable, making it suitable for both small businesses and large enterprises. Whether you need to collect data from a handful of respondents or thousands, Microsoft Forms can handle the load efficiently. This scalability ensures that as your organization grows, your data collection needs can continue to be met without requiring a change in tools. Additionally, the ability to create forms in multiple languages supports global operations and facilitates data collection from diverse audiences.

11. Cost-Effectiveness

For organizations already using Microsoft 365, Microsoft Forms is included as part of the subscription, making it a cost-effective solution for data collection. This eliminates the need for investing in additional survey tools and reduces overall operational costs. Even for those not using Microsoft 365, the availability of a free version with essential features makes it accessible to a wide range of users.

12. Continuous Improvement

Microsoft continuously updates and improves Microsoft Forms based on user feedback and technological advancements. These updates often include new features, enhanced security measures, and improved performance, ensuring that users always have access to the latest capabilities. This commitment to continuous improvement means that users can rely on Microsoft Forms to meet their evolving needs and expectations over time.

13. Educational Benefits

Microsoft Forms is particularly beneficial in educational settings. Educators can use the tool to create quizzes, surveys, and polls to engage students, assess learning, and gather feedback. The ability to provide instant feedback on quizzes helps reinforce learning, while the data collected from surveys can inform instructional practices and improve the overall educational experience. The integration with Microsoft Teams further supports collaborative learning environments.

14. Enhanced Engagement

Engagement is a key factor in the success of any form or survey. Microsoft Forms enhances engagement through its interactive features, such as branching logic, which customizes the respondent's experience based on their answers. This personalization makes the form more relevant and interesting to the respondent, increasing the likelihood of completion. Additionally, the ability to add multimedia elements, such as images and videos, captures respondents' attention and keeps them engaged throughout the form.

15. Feedback and Continuous Improvement

Using Microsoft Forms for feedback collection allows organizations to continuously improve their processes, products, and services. By gathering feedback from customers, employees, or other stakeholders, organizations can identify areas for improvement and implement changes that enhance satisfaction and performance. The ease of creating and distributing forms ensures that feedback can be collected regularly, fostering a culture of continuous improvement.

In conclusion, Microsoft Forms offers a multitude of benefits that make it an invaluable tool for data collection, analysis, and decision-making. Its user-friendly interface, versatility, integration capabilities, and robust security features make it suitable for a wide range of applications across different industries. Whether you are looking to create simple surveys or complex quizzes, Microsoft Forms provides the functionality and flexibility needed to achieve your goals effectively.

1.2 Getting Started with Microsoft Forms

1.2.1 Accessing Microsoft Forms

Microsoft Forms is a powerful and user-friendly tool designed for creating surveys, quizzes, and polls. To leverage its full potential, you need to know how to access and navigate the platform effectively. This section will guide you through the various methods of accessing Microsoft Forms and ensure you can start creating your forms and quizzes with ease.

Accessing Microsoft Forms via Web Browser

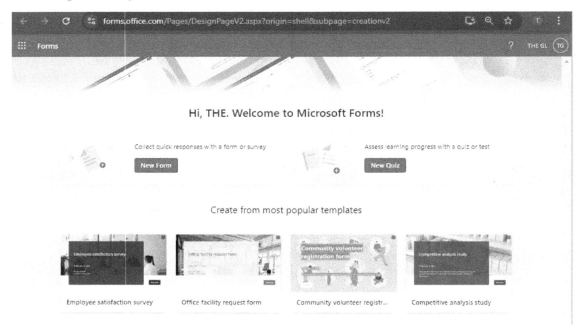

The most common method to access Microsoft Forms is through a web browser. Follow these steps:

1. Open Your Web Browser: Microsoft Forms is compatible with all major web browsers, including Google Chrome, Mozilla Firefox, Microsoft Edge, and Safari. Ensure that your browser is updated to the latest version to avoid any compatibility issues.

2. Navigate to the Microsoft Forms Website: Type `forms.microsoft.com` into your browser's address bar and press Enter. This will direct you to the Microsoft Forms homepage.

3. Sign In to Your Microsoft Account: To access Microsoft Forms, you need to sign in with your Microsoft account. If you are already signed in, you will be taken directly to the Forms dashboard. If not, you will be prompted to enter your email address and password associated with your Microsoft account.

4. Access Your Forms and Quizzes: Once signed in, you will see the Forms dashboard. Here, you can view all your existing forms and quizzes. If this is your first time using Microsoft Forms, the dashboard will be empty except for a welcome message and options to create new forms or quizzes.

Accessing Microsoft Forms via Microsoft 365

If you are a Microsoft 365 subscriber, you can access Microsoft Forms through your Microsoft 365 account. Here's how:

1. Log In to Microsoft 365: Open your web browser and go to `office.com`. Enter your Microsoft 365 credentials to sign in. If you are part of an organization, you may use your organizational account.

2. Open the Microsoft 365 App Launcher: After logging in, you will be taken to the Microsoft 365 home page. Click on the App Launcher icon (a grid of dots) located in the upper-left corner of the page.

3. Select Microsoft Forms: From the App Launcher menu, click on the Microsoft Forms icon. This will redirect you to the Forms application where you can start creating and managing your forms and quizzes.

Accessing Microsoft Forms via Mobile Apps

Microsoft Forms is also accessible via mobile apps, which can be particularly useful for managing your forms on the go. Here's how to access Microsoft Forms on your mobile device:

1. Download the Microsoft Forms App: As of now, Microsoft Forms does not have a standalone mobile app. Instead, it can be accessed through the Microsoft Office app, available on both iOS and Android devices.

2. Install the Microsoft Office App: Go to the App Store (for iOS devices) or Google Play Store (for Android devices) and search for "Microsoft Office." Download and install the app.

3. Sign In to Your Microsoft Account: Open the Microsoft Office app and sign in with your Microsoft account credentials.

4. Access Microsoft Forms: Once signed in, navigate to the Forms section within the app. You will have access to your existing forms and quizzes and can create new ones directly from your mobile device.

Accessing Microsoft Forms through Microsoft Teams

For users who are part of an organization that uses Microsoft Teams, integrating Microsoft Forms within Teams can enhance collaboration and streamline form management. Here's how to access Microsoft Forms through Microsoft Teams:

1. Open Microsoft Teams: Launch Microsoft Teams on your desktop or mobile device. Sign in with your organizational account if prompted.

2. Navigate to the Teams Channel: Go to the specific channel within your team where you want to create or manage forms.

3. Add Microsoft Forms Tab: Click on the "+" icon at the top of the channel to add a new tab. Select "Forms" from the list of available apps.

4. Create or Access Forms: You can either create a new form or quiz directly from the Teams tab or access existing ones. This integration allows for easy sharing and collaboration with your team members.

Accessing Microsoft Forms via SharePoint

If your organization uses SharePoint, you can integrate Microsoft Forms into SharePoint sites for easy access and management. Follow these steps:

1. Open SharePoint: Go to your SharePoint site where you want to add a form.

2. Add a Microsoft Forms Web Part: Navigate to the page where you want to embed the form. Click "Edit" to modify the page, then click on the "+" icon to add a new web part.

3. Select Microsoft Forms: Choose the Microsoft Forms web part from the list of available web parts.

4. Embed Your Form: You can either create a new form or link an existing one. This allows users to access and fill out the form directly from the SharePoint site.

Troubleshooting Access Issues

Occasionally, users may encounter issues accessing Microsoft Forms. Here are some common problems and solutions:

1. Browser Issues: Ensure that your web browser is up-to-date and that cookies and JavaScript are enabled. Clearing your browser's cache may also resolve access issues.

2. Account Problems: Verify that you are signed in with the correct Microsoft account. If you are part of an organization, check that your account has the necessary permissions to access Microsoft Forms.

3. Network Problems: Ensure that you have a stable internet connection. If you are on a corporate network, firewall settings may sometimes restrict access to certain features.

4. Service Outages: Occasionally, Microsoft Forms may experience service disruptions. Check the Microsoft 365 Service Status page for any ongoing issues that may be affecting access.

Conclusion

Accessing Microsoft Forms is straightforward, whether you are using a web browser, Microsoft 365, mobile apps, Microsoft Teams, or SharePoint. Understanding these access methods ensures that you can effectively utilize Microsoft Forms for creating surveys, quizzes, and polls, regardless of the platform you prefer. By mastering these access techniques, you can streamline your workflow and enhance your ability to collect and analyze data efficiently.

This comprehensive guide to accessing Microsoft Forms will serve as a foundation for exploring more advanced features and functionalities in the subsequent sections of this book.

1.2.2 Creating a Microsoft Account

Creating a Microsoft Account is the first step to accessing and using Microsoft Forms. This account is your gateway to a range of Microsoft services and products, including Microsoft Forms. Below, we'll walk through the process of setting up a Microsoft Account, explore the various options available, and address common questions and concerns.

Understanding the Microsoft Account

A Microsoft Account is a unified user account that provides access to a variety of Microsoft services such as Outlook, OneDrive, Office 365, and Microsoft Forms. By creating a Microsoft Account, you gain access to these services with a single set of credentials. This account is essential for utilizing Microsoft Forms, as it allows you to create, manage, and share forms seamlessly.

Steps to Create a Microsoft Account

1. Visit the Microsoft Account Sign-Up Page

To begin the process, open your web browser and navigate to the Microsoft Account sign-up page: signup.live.com. This page will guide you through creating a new account.

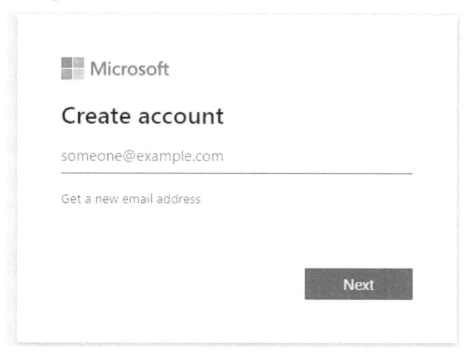

2. Provide Your Email Address

On the sign-up page, you'll be prompted to enter an email address. You can use an existing email address from another provider (such as Gmail or Yahoo), or you can create a new Outlook.com email address.

- Using an Existing Email Address: Enter your preferred email address and click "Next." Microsoft will send a verification code to this email address to confirm its validity.

- Creating a New Outlook Address: If you prefer to create a new email address with Microsoft, select "Get a new email address." Choose a username and domain (e.g., @outlook.com or @hotmail.com), and then click "Next."

3. Create a Password

Next, you'll need to create a password for your new Microsoft Account. This password should be strong and secure, ideally comprising a mix of upper and lower case letters, numbers, and special characters. Microsoft will provide guidelines to help you create a secure password.

4. Enter Your Personal Information

You'll be asked to provide some basic personal information, including:

- Full Name: Enter your first and last name.

- Country/Region: Select your country or region from the drop-down menu.

- Date of Birth: Input your birthdate to verify your age and comply with legal requirements.

5. Verify Your Identity

To ensure that you're a real person and not a bot, Microsoft will ask you to verify your identity. This is typically done via a verification code sent to your email address or phone number. Enter the code you receive to complete the verification process.

6. Agree to the Terms and Conditions

Carefully review Microsoft's Terms of Use and Privacy Statement. These documents outline your rights and responsibilities as a user of Microsoft services. Once you've read and understood these terms, check the box to agree and click "Create account."

7. Complete the Setup

After creating your account, you may be prompted to set up additional security features such as two-step verification. This step is optional but recommended for enhancing the security of your account.

Configuring Your Microsoft Account

Once your account is created, you can configure various settings to personalize your experience and ensure optimal security:

1. Personalize Your Account

- Profile Information: Update your profile with additional details such as a profile picture and contact information.

- Security Settings: Review and adjust your security settings, including setting up two-step verification and security questions.

- Privacy Settings: Manage your privacy preferences to control what information you share and with whom.

2. Sync with Other Devices

Microsoft Accounts offer the benefit of syncing your settings and data across multiple devices. If you're using Windows 10 or later, your Microsoft Account will sync settings like themes, passwords, and preferences across all your devices.

3. Explore Microsoft Services

With your Microsoft Account set up, you can now access a wide range of Microsoft services:

- Outlook: Manage your emails, calendars, and contacts.

- OneDrive: Store and share files in the cloud.

- Office 365: Access productivity tools such as Word, Excel, and PowerPoint.

- Microsoft Forms: Start creating and managing forms and quizzes.

Common Questions and Troubleshooting

1. What if I Forget My Password?

If you forget your password, you can reset it by clicking the "Forgot my password" link on the sign-in page. Follow the prompts to verify your identity and create a new password.

2. Can I Use a Corporate Email Address?

Yes, you can use a corporate email address to create a Microsoft Account. However, some features might be restricted based on your organization's policies.

3. How Do I Recover a Disabled Account?

If your account is disabled, you'll need to contact Microsoft Support for assistance. They can help you recover your account if it's been disabled due to inactivity or security concerns.

4. Is Two-Step Verification Necessary?

While not mandatory, two-step verification adds an extra layer of security to your account by requiring a second form of authentication. This is highly recommended to protect your account from unauthorized access.

Conclusion

Creating a Microsoft Account is a straightforward process that unlocks a world of Microsoft services, including Microsoft Forms. By following the steps outlined above, you'll be able to set up your account quickly and efficiently. Once your account is active, you can begin exploring the full range of features available in Microsoft Forms, from designing surveys and quizzes to analyzing responses.

A well-configured Microsoft Account not only enhances your experience with Microsoft Forms but also integrates seamlessly with other Microsoft tools, providing a cohesive and productive digital environment.

1.2.3 Navigating the Microsoft Forms Interface

Microsoft Forms is designed with an intuitive and user-friendly interface that allows both novice and experienced users to create, distribute, and analyze surveys and quizzes with ease. In this section, we will explore the various elements of the Microsoft Forms interface, guiding you through each component to ensure you can efficiently navigate and utilize the platform's features.

The Dashboard Overview

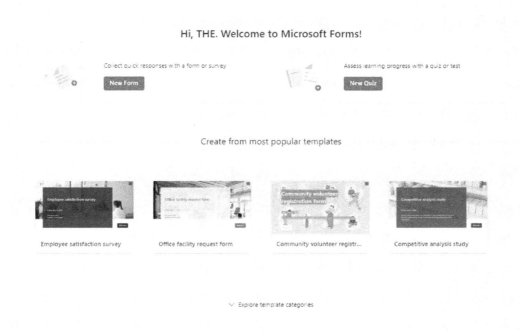

When you first log into Microsoft Forms, you are greeted with the dashboard, which serves as the central hub for all your form-related activities. The dashboard is divided into several key areas:

- My Forms: This section displays all the forms and quizzes you have created. Each form is represented by a tile that shows the form's title, a thumbnail preview, and the number of responses collected. You can sort and filter your forms based on various criteria, such as the date of creation or the number of responses.

- Shared with Me: Forms that have been shared with you by other users appear in this section. This is particularly useful for collaborative projects, where multiple team members contribute to the creation and management of forms. You can view and edit these forms if you have been granted the appropriate permissions.

- Recent Forms: This section provides quick access to the forms you have most recently worked on. It's a convenient way to jump back into a form you were editing or analyzing without needing to search for it in the My Forms section.

- Templates: Microsoft Forms offers a range of pre-designed templates that you can use as a starting point for your surveys or quizzes. These templates are categorized based on their intended use, such as education, business, or event planning. Using a template can save you time and provide inspiration for how to structure your own forms.

- New Form and New Quiz: These buttons are prominently displayed on the dashboard, allowing you to quickly create a new form or quiz. Clicking on either button takes you directly to the form creation interface.

The Form Creation Interface

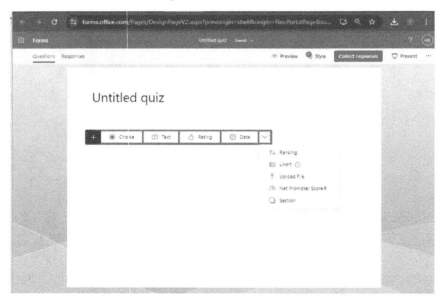

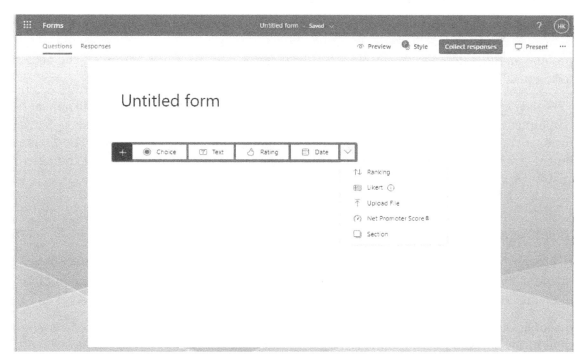

The form creation interface is where you will spend most of your time in Microsoft Forms. This interface is designed to be both simple and powerful, providing you with all the tools you need to design and customize your forms. The interface is divided into several key areas:

- Title and Description Area: At the top of the form creation interface, you'll find the title and description fields. The title is the first thing respondents will see, so it's important to make it clear and descriptive. The description field allows you to provide additional context or instructions for your respondents, helping them understand the purpose of the form or how to complete it.

- Form Body: The main area of the interface is the form body, where you will add and organize your questions. This area is highly flexible, allowing you to drag and drop questions to rearrange their order, add sections to group related questions, and insert various types of content, such as images or videos, to enhance your form.

- Question Types Toolbar: Located on the right side of the form body, the question types toolbar is where you'll find all the available question types you can add to your form. These include multiple choice, text, rating, date, and more. Each question type is represented by an icon, and clicking on an icon will insert a new question of that type into the form body.

- Settings and Options: Above the form body, you'll find a toolbar with various settings and options for your form. These include the ability to toggle between different views (e.g., preview mode), adjust form settings (e.g., branching logic, response settings), and access form-specific features (e.g., themes, sharing options).

- Preview and Themes: The preview button allows you to see how your form will appear to respondents on different devices, such as desktops, tablets, or smartphones. This is crucial for ensuring that your form is user-friendly and accessible on all platforms. The themes button opens a panel where you can choose from a variety of pre-designed themes or customize the colors and fonts to match your brand or personal preference.

Working with Questions

Questions are the heart of any survey or quiz, and Microsoft Forms offers a range of question types to suit different needs. Understanding how to add, edit, and organize questions is key to creating effective forms.

- Adding Questions: To add a question to your form, simply click on the desired question type in the question types toolbar. A new question will be inserted into the form body, where you can enter your question text, specify answer options, and adjust settings such as whether the question is required.

- Editing Questions: Each question in your form comes with its own set of customization options. Depending on the question type, you can add or remove answer choices, set default answers, add question branching, or provide additional instructions or hints. The editing options appear directly below the question text in the form body, making it easy to make adjustments as you work.

- Organizing Questions: Microsoft Forms allows you to easily reorganize your questions by dragging and dropping them within the form body. You can also use sections to group related questions together, which can help structure your form logically and make it easier for respondents to follow.

- Question Settings: For each question, you can access additional settings by clicking the ellipsis (three dots) next to the question. These settings include options like shuffling answer choices (useful for multiple-choice questions), adding subtitles, or providing answer validation (e.g., setting a minimum or maximum number of characters for text responses).

Managing Form Settings

Once you have added and organized your questions, you may want to customize the overall settings for your form. Microsoft Forms offers several options that allow you to control how respondents interact with your form and how the data is collected.

- Response Settings: In the form settings menu, you can specify who can respond to your form (e.g., anyone with the link, or only people within your organization) and whether respondents can submit multiple responses. You can also set start and end dates for when the form is available, limit the number of responses, and provide respondents with a custom thank-you message upon submission.

- Branching Logic: Branching allows you to create dynamic forms that change based on respondents' answers. For example, if a respondent selects a particular answer, you can direct them to a different set of questions or skip certain sections altogether. Branching is set up in the form settings menu, where you can define the logic for each question and determine how respondents are directed through the form.

- Notifications: Microsoft Forms can send you an email notification each time someone submits a response. This is particularly useful for forms that require immediate attention, such as feedback forms or incident reports. You can enable or disable email notifications in the form settings menu.

Previewing and Testing Your Form

Before sharing your form with respondents, it's important to preview and test it to ensure everything works as intended. Microsoft Forms provides several tools to help you with this process.

- Preview Mode: Clicking the preview button allows you to see your form exactly as your respondents will. You can switch between different device views (e.g., desktop, tablet, mobile) to check that your form is responsive and looks good on all screens. While in preview mode, you can also test out the form by entering sample responses, which can help you catch any issues with question logic or formatting.

- Testing Branching Logic: If your form uses branching logic, it's crucial to test it thoroughly to ensure that respondents are directed to the correct questions based on their answers. In preview mode, you can simulate different response scenarios and observe how the form behaves, allowing you to make any necessary adjustments before the form goes live.

Sharing and Distributing Your Form

Once you're satisfied with your form, the final step is to share it with your intended audience. Microsoft Forms offers several methods for distributing your form, making it easy to reach respondents wherever they are.

- Sharing via Link: The most common way to share a Microsoft Form is via a direct link. In the share menu, you'll find a unique URL that you can copy and distribute through email, social media, or any other platform. You can also customize the link settings, such as allowing anyone with the link to respond or restricting access to specific users.

- Embedding in a Website: If you have a website or blog, you can embed your form directly into a webpage. The share menu provides an embed code that you can paste into your website's HTML. This allows respondents to complete the form without leaving your site, which can lead to higher response rates.

- QR Code: For situations where a printed form or mobile distribution is preferred, Microsoft Forms allows you to generate a QR code that links to your form. Respondents can scan the code with their smartphones to access the form instantly.

- Sharing via Email: You can also send your form directly via email using the built-in email distribution feature. This method embeds the form link in an email template, making it easy to send out to your contact list.

Monitoring Responses and Analyzing Data

After your form has been distributed, Microsoft Forms provides robust tools for monitoring responses and analyzing the data you collect.

- Real-Time Response Monitoring: The responses tab in the form creation interface displays real-time data as respondents submit their answers. You can see an overview of the number of responses, response rates, and other key metrics. This real-time monitoring allows you to keep track of how your form is performing and make any necessary adjustments.

- Data Visualization: Microsoft Forms automatically generates visualizations for your response data, such as charts and graphs. These visualizations help you quickly interpret the results and identify trends. You can view data for individual questions or analyze the overall response patterns.

- Exporting Data: For more in-depth analysis, you can export your response data to Excel. This allows you to perform advanced data manipulation, create custom reports, and integrate your data with other applications. The export feature ensures that you have full control over your data and can use it in ways that best meet your needs.

Conclusion

Navigating the Microsoft Forms interface is a crucial step in mastering the tool and creating effective surveys and quizzes. By familiarizing yourself with the dashboard, form creation interface, and various settings and features, you can streamline your workflow and produce forms that are both functional and visually appealing. Whether you are creating a simple feedback form or a complex quiz with branching logic, the skills you develop in navigating the Microsoft Forms interface will serve as the foundation for all your future projects.

CHAPTER II
Creating Your First Form

2.1 Designing Your Form

Designing a form is one of the most crucial steps in using Microsoft Forms effectively. A well-designed form not only captures the necessary information but also ensures that respondents find it easy and intuitive to complete. In this section, we will explore the process of selecting a template, which serves as the foundation of your form's design.

2.1.1 Selecting a Template

Introduction to Templates

When you first start creating a form in Microsoft Forms, one of the key decisions you'll make is whether to begin with a blank form or use a pre-designed template. Templates in Microsoft Forms are pre-configured structures that provide a starting point for your survey or quiz. They are designed to save you time by offering layouts and question types that are commonly used for specific purposes, such as feedback surveys, event registrations, or quizzes. Selecting the right template can streamline the creation process and ensure that your form meets its intended purpose effectively.

Why Use Templates?

Templates are incredibly useful for several reasons:

- Time Efficiency: Templates save time by providing a pre-set structure that you can customize rather than starting from scratch.

- Best Practices: They incorporate best practices in form design, such as question phrasing, order, and layout, which can enhance respondent engagement.

- Consistency: Using templates helps maintain consistency across multiple forms, which is particularly beneficial in a business or educational setting where uniformity is important.

- Guidance: For those who are new to form creation, templates offer guidance by demonstrating effective ways to structure questions and organize content.

Types of Templates Available in Microsoft Forms

Microsoft Forms offers a variety of templates designed to meet different needs. These templates are categorized to help you quickly find the most relevant one for your purpose. Some common categories include:

1. Feedback Forms: Templates designed for collecting feedback, such as customer satisfaction surveys, employee engagement surveys, or product feedback forms.

2. Event Registrations: These templates are structured to gather information from participants for events like webinars, workshops, or conferences. They typically include fields for names, contact details, and preferences.

3. Quizzes and Assessments: Designed for educational purposes, these templates are useful for creating quizzes, exams, or self-assessments. They often include various question types like multiple-choice, true/false, and short answer.

4. Polls: Templates for quick polls are ideal for gathering opinions or preferences from a group. These are often used in meetings or webinars to engage participants.

5. Sign-Up Sheets: These templates facilitate the collection of sign-ups for activities, shifts, or volunteer opportunities. They include fields for names, availability, and specific preferences.

How to Select and Use a Template

Selecting a template in Microsoft Forms is a straightforward process, but it's important to understand how to choose the right one for your specific needs. Here's a step-by-step guide:

1. Accessing Templates: After logging into Microsoft Forms, you'll be directed to the homepage. To start a new form using a template, click on the "New Form" button. This will bring up the option to choose a template or start from scratch.

2. Browsing Templates: Microsoft Forms categorizes templates by purpose, making it easier to browse through the options. Categories such as "Education," "Business," and "Health" allow you to filter templates based on your specific industry or need. You can also use the search bar to find templates by keywords.

3. Previewing Templates: Before selecting a template, you can preview it to see the structure, question types, and overall layout. This preview feature helps you evaluate whether the template aligns with your needs.

4. Customizing the Template: Once you've selected a template, you can customize it to suit your specific requirements. This might involve adding or removing questions, changing the wording of questions, or adjusting the layout. Microsoft Forms allows a high degree of customization, so you can tailor the template to your exact needs.

5. Saving and Reusing Custom Templates: If you create a form that you think you might use again in the future, you can save it as a custom template. This feature is particularly useful for businesses and educators who need to create similar forms repeatedly. Saving a custom template allows you to start from a familiar place each time, reducing setup time and ensuring consistency across forms.

Best Practices for Template Selection

When choosing a template, consider the following best practices to ensure that your form is as effective as possible:

1. Purpose Alignment: Ensure the template aligns with the specific purpose of your form. For instance, a customer feedback template is structured differently from a quiz template, as they are designed to meet different objectives.

2. Simplicity: Choose a template that is straightforward and easy to navigate. Overly complex templates can confuse respondents and lead to incomplete submissions.

3. Customization Capability: Consider how easily you can customize the template to meet your specific needs. Some templates are more rigid in structure, while others offer more flexibility.

4. Audience Appropriateness: Select a template that is appropriate for your target audience. For example, a template designed for a student quiz might not be suitable for a corporate feedback survey.

5. Response Type Suitability: Different templates support various response types (e.g., multiple-choice, open-ended, rating scales). Ensure the template you select allows you to collect the type of data you need.

Example Scenarios of Template Use

Here are a few scenarios where selecting the right template can make a significant difference in the effectiveness of your form:

- Educational Quiz: A teacher wants to create a quiz to assess student understanding of a recently covered topic. Using a "Quiz" template allows the teacher to easily include a variety of question types, such as multiple-choice and short answer, and automatically grade responses.

- Customer Feedback Survey: A small business owner wants to gather feedback from customers after they've made a purchase. By selecting a "Customer Feedback" template, the owner can quickly create a survey that includes relevant questions about product satisfaction, service experience, and suggestions for improvement.

- Event Registration: An event planner needs to gather information from attendees for an upcoming conference. The "Event Registration" template offers a structured way to collect contact information, session preferences, and dietary requirements, ensuring all necessary details are captured efficiently.

- Employee Engagement Survey: An HR manager wants to gauge employee satisfaction and gather suggestions for workplace improvement. The "Employee Engagement" template provides a balanced mix of rating scales, open-ended questions, and demographic fields, making it easy to gather comprehensive feedback.

Conclusion

Selecting a template is a foundational step in the form creation process in Microsoft Forms. By choosing the right template, you can save time, ensure consistency, and leverage best practices in form design. Microsoft Forms offers a variety of templates tailored to different purposes, making it easy to find one that suits your needs. Whether you are conducting a survey, creating a quiz, or gathering event registrations, starting with a template can set you on the right path to creating an effective and engaging form. Remember to customize the template to match your specific requirements and to consider your audience and data collection needs during the selection process.

2.1.2 Customizing the Form Layout

Customizing the layout of your form is a crucial step in creating an engaging and user-friendly experience for respondents. A well-designed form not only looks aesthetically pleasing but also ensures that the respondents can navigate and complete the form with ease. In this section, we will explore various customization options available in Microsoft Forms to help you tailor your form to meet specific needs and preferences.

1. Form Structure and Organization

The structure of your form plays a significant role in how respondents perceive and interact with it. Here are some tips for organizing your form effectively:

- Use Sections and Pages: Break your form into logical sections or pages to prevent overwhelming respondents with too many questions at once. This approach helps in maintaining focus and improving response rates.

- Group Related Questions: Place similar or related questions together. For example, demographic questions can be grouped at the beginning, while specific survey questions can follow.

- Use Descriptive Titles and Subheadings: Clearly label each section and provide subheadings where necessary to guide respondents through the form.

2. Themes and Colors

Microsoft Forms offers a variety of themes and color schemes to enhance the visual appeal of your form. Customizing the theme and colors can help align the form with your organization's branding or the specific context of the survey.

- Applying Themes: Choose from pre-defined themes that include background images and color palettes. To apply a theme, go to the "Theme" button at the top of the form editor, and select a theme that suits your needs.

- Custom Colors: If the available themes don't match your requirements, you can customize the colors manually. Click on the "Customize Theme" option, where you can choose colors for the background, question text, and response options.

- Background Images: Adding a background image can make your form more visually appealing. Ensure the image is relevant and does not distract from the questions. You can upload your own image or select one from the Microsoft Forms library.

3. Fonts and Text Styling

The readability of your form is influenced by the fonts and text styles you use. Microsoft Forms allows some degree of customization in this area:

- Font Selection: While the options are somewhat limited compared to other design tools, you can choose from a few different font styles to match the tone of your form.

- Text Size and Formatting: Ensure that your text is legible by adjusting the size and using formatting options like bold, italics, and underlining where necessary. For instance, use bold text for section titles and question headings to make them stand out.

4. Question Alignment and Spacing

Proper alignment and spacing contribute to the overall cleanliness and readability of your form. Consider the following:

- Aligning Questions: Align questions consistently, either left-aligned or center-aligned, based on the design aesthetic you are aiming for.

- Spacing Between Questions: Maintain adequate spacing between questions to avoid a cluttered appearance. Too much white space, however, can make the form appear sparse, so find a balance.

5. Customizing Question Layouts

Different types of questions may require different layouts to optimize respondent interaction:

- Multiple Choice Questions: Present multiple-choice questions in a single column for easy scanning. If there are many options, consider using a dropdown menu to save space.

- Text Questions: For open-ended text questions, provide ample space for respondents to type their answers. Use multiline text boxes for questions that require longer responses.

- Rating Questions: Display rating scales horizontally for a more intuitive layout. Ensure that the rating scale labels are clear and easy to understand.

- Date Questions: Use a date picker to simplify the process of entering dates. This can help prevent formatting errors and improve accuracy.

6. Adding Visual Elements

Visual elements like images and videos can enhance the form's engagement and provide additional context for respondents:

- Images: Insert images to illustrate questions or provide visual cues. Ensure that images are relevant and of high quality. Use the "Insert Image" option available in the question settings.

- Videos: Embed videos to provide instructions or additional information related to the form. Videos can be particularly useful in educational or training contexts. Use the "Insert Video" option and provide a YouTube or Stream URL.

7. Using Form Branching

Form branching allows you to create dynamic forms that change based on respondents' answers. This feature helps in tailoring the form experience and gathering more relevant data:

- Setting Up Branching: To set up branching, go to the "More settings for question" option (three dots) and select "Add branching." Here, you can specify which question respondents should be directed to based on their previous answers.

- Creating Conditional Paths: Use conditional paths to skip irrelevant questions or guide respondents through different sections of the form. For example, if a respondent selects "No" to a question about prior experience, you can skip subsequent detailed questions about that experience.

8. Previewing and Testing Your Form

Before finalizing your form, it's essential to preview and test it to ensure everything looks and works as intended:

- Preview Mode: Use the "Preview" button to see how your form will appear on different devices, including desktops, tablets, and smartphones. This helps in identifying any layout issues or adjustments needed.

- Test Responses: Fill out the form yourself to test the flow and functionality. Check for any errors in branching, question alignment, or data collection settings.

9. Accessibility Considerations

Ensuring your form is accessible to all respondents, including those with disabilities, is important for inclusivity:

- Screen Reader Compatibility: Design your form to be compatible with screen readers by providing clear and descriptive text for all questions and options.

- Keyboard Navigation: Ensure that all form elements can be navigated and completed using a keyboard.

- Color Contrast: Use high-contrast color schemes to make the text readable for respondents with visual impairments. Avoid using color alone to convey information.

10. Saving and Sharing Your Customized Form

Once you have customized the layout of your form, save your work and share it with your target audience:

- Saving Your Form: Microsoft Forms saves changes automatically, but it's a good practice to periodically check that all customizations are applied correctly.

- Sharing Options: Share your form via a link, email, QR code, or by embedding it on a website. You can adjust the sharing settings to control who can respond (anyone with the link or only people within your organization).

By following these steps and utilizing the customization options available in Microsoft Forms, you can create a well-structured, visually appealing, and user-friendly form that effectively gathers the data you need.

2.2 Adding Questions and Content

Adding questions and content to your form is the heart of the Microsoft Forms experience. This section will guide you through the process of selecting the right types of questions, organizing them effectively, and enriching your form with additional content such as images and videos. By mastering these skills, you'll be able to create forms that are not only functional but also engaging and visually appealing to your respondents.

2.2.1 Types of Questions

When constructing a form in Microsoft Forms, the choice of question types is crucial. The types of questions you include will determine how effectively you can gather the information you need, how easy it is for respondents to provide that information, and how you can analyze the responses later. Microsoft Forms offers several question types, each suited to different kinds of data collection. Below, we will explore the main types of questions you can add to your form: Multiple Choice, Text, Rating, and Date.

2.2.1.1 Multiple Choice

The Multiple Choice question type is one of the most versatile and widely used in Microsoft Forms. It allows respondents to select one or more options from a predefined list of answers. This question type is particularly useful for gathering categorical data, where you want respondents to choose from a set list of possibilities.

Creating a Multiple Choice Question:

To create a Multiple Choice question, start by selecting the "Choice" option from the question type dropdown. You can then enter your question in the provided field and add as many answer choices as you need. Each choice can be edited to include rich text or hyperlinks if needed.

Single-Selection vs. Multiple-Selection:

By default, the Multiple Choice question allows only one answer to be selected (single-selection). However, you can enable the "Multiple answers" option if you want respondents to select more than one choice. This is useful in scenarios where multiple responses are valid, such as selecting all applicable features or preferences.

Advanced Options:

- Shuffle Options: You can choose to shuffle the order of the answer choices for each respondent, which helps to reduce bias in responses.

- Add 'Other' Option: If you want to allow respondents to provide an answer that is not listed, you can add an "Other" option where they can type their response.

- Required Field: You can make the question mandatory by toggling the "Required" option, ensuring that respondents cannot submit the form without answering the question.

Use Cases for Multiple Choice Questions:

- Feedback Forms: For gathering opinions or feedback where predefined options are sufficient.

- Quizzes: To test knowledge with clear, correct answers.

- Polls and Surveys: Where you need to gauge preferences or opinions from a list of options.

2.2.1.2 Text

The Text question type is designed to capture open-ended responses. It provides respondents with a text box where they can type their answers. This type of question is ideal for collecting qualitative data, opinions, explanations, or any other type of input that doesn't fit into predefined categories.

Creating a Text Question:

To add a Text question, select the "Text" option from the question type dropdown. You can then enter your question or prompt in the designated field.

Short Answer vs. Long Answer:

Microsoft Forms offers two variants of the Text question:

- Short Answer: This is a single-line text box suitable for brief responses, such as names, email addresses, or short comments.

- Long Answer: If you anticipate longer responses, you can enable the "Long Answer" option, which provides a larger text area. This is ideal for questions that require detailed explanations or descriptions.

Advanced Options:

- Restrict Answer Length: You can limit the number of characters or words that respondents can enter, which is useful for controlling the scope of responses.

- Regular Expressions: For more technical users, Microsoft Forms supports the use of regular expressions to validate text input, ensuring that responses meet specific formatting criteria (e.g., email addresses, phone numbers).

Use Cases for Text Questions:

- Feedback and Suggestions: Allowing respondents to express their thoughts in their own words.

- Descriptive Responses: Collecting detailed descriptions, such as when asking about experiences or opinions.

- Open-Ended Surveys: Where the goal is to gather a wide range of responses without limiting options.

2.2.1.3 Rating

The Rating question type allows respondents to evaluate a particular item or statement on a scale, such as from 1 to 5 or 1 to 10. This is particularly useful when you want to measure sentiment, satisfaction, or agreement on a linear scale.

Creating a Rating Question:

To create a Rating question, select "Rating" from the question type dropdown. You can then enter your question or statement that you want respondents to evaluate.

Choosing a Rating Scale:

- Stars or Numbers: Microsoft Forms gives you the option to use stars (commonly used for ratings) or numbers to represent the scale.

- Scale Length: You can choose the length of the scale, typically ranging from 1 to 5 or 1 to 10. The choice of scale depends on how granular you want the feedback to be.

Advanced Options:

- Labeling the Scale: You can add labels to the minimum and maximum points on the scale to clarify what each end represents (e.g., 1 = Poor, 5 = Excellent).

- Required Field: Like other question types, you can make this question mandatory to ensure that respondents provide a rating.

Use Cases for Rating Questions:

- Customer Satisfaction Surveys: To gauge overall satisfaction with a product or service.

- Performance Evaluations: For assessing aspects such as employee performance or event success.

- Opinion Polls: When you want respondents to express their level of agreement or preference.

2.2.1.4 Date

The Date question type is used to capture specific dates from respondents. This can be useful in forms where you need to know when something occurred or when a respondent plans to do something in the future.

Creating a Date Question:

To add a Date question, select "Date" from the question type dropdown. You can then specify your question or prompt.

Date Format and Range:

- Default Format: The date format will typically align with the respondent's regional settings, ensuring that it's displayed in a familiar format.

- Date Ranges: Although Microsoft Forms doesn't natively support limiting the date range, you can use the question text to instruct respondents to enter a date within a specific range.

Advanced Options:

- Date and Time: If you need more precision, you can prompt respondents to provide both the date and time, although this requires an additional question or clarification within the text question.

Use Cases for Date Questions:

- Event Planning: Collecting dates for scheduling or attendance purposes.

- Surveys: Gathering data on when specific events or experiences occurred.

- Appointments: For booking or confirming meeting dates.

By effectively utilizing the various types of questions and media available in Microsoft Forms, you can create a form that is not only functional but also engaging and informative. The next section will guide you through setting additional options for your form to further customize its behavior and how respondents interact with it.

2.2.2 Adding Media to Your Form

Incorporating media elements such as images and videos into your forms can significantly enhance the user experience, making your surveys and quizzes more engaging, informative, and visually appealing. Media can help clarify questions, provide additional context, or simply make the form more interactive. In this section, we will explore the steps and best practices for adding images and videos to your Microsoft Forms.

2.2.2.1 Images

Why Use Images in Forms?

Images can serve multiple purposes in a form. They can help clarify a question, provide visual examples, make the form more engaging, or simply break up the monotony of text. For instance, in a survey about product feedback, images of the products can help respondents easily identify what they are being asked about. Similarly, in educational quizzes, images can be used to illustrate concepts or test visual recognition skills.

Adding Images to Your Questions

To add an image to a question in Microsoft Forms, follow these steps:

1. Select the Question: Click on the question where you want to add an image. This could be any question type, such as multiple choice, text, or rating.

2. Click on the Image Icon: In the question editor, you'll see an image icon (a small picture symbol). Click on this icon to add an image to your question.

3. Choose the Image Source: Microsoft Forms allows you to upload images from different sources:

   - Upload from Your Device: You can upload an image directly from your computer or mobile device. This is useful for adding custom images, such as logos, product pictures, or infographics.

   - Search the Web: You can use Bing's image search to find and add images directly from the web. This is helpful if you need general images or visuals that you do not have saved on your device.

   - OneDrive: If you have images stored in your OneDrive account, you can easily add them to your form by selecting the OneDrive option.

   - Recent: This option lets you quickly access and insert images you have recently used in other forms or documents.

4. Adjust the Image Placement: Once the image is added, you can adjust its placement and size. You may want to align the image above the question text or alongside it, depending on the layout that best suits your form's design.

5. Add Alt Text: To ensure your form is accessible to all users, including those using screen readers, it's important to add alt text to your images. Alt text describes the image content and can be added by clicking on the image and selecting the "Alt Text" option.

Best Practices for Using Images

- Relevance: Ensure that every image you include is relevant to the question or content it accompanies. Irrelevant images can confuse respondents and reduce the clarity of your form.

- Size and Quality: Use high-quality images that are clear and easy to see. However, be mindful of file sizes; large images can slow down the form's loading time, especially on mobile devices.

- Consistency: Maintain a consistent style for all images used within a single form. This could involve using images of similar sizes, styles, or colors, which helps create a cohesive and professional look.

Examples of Using Images in Forms

- Product Feedback: Include images of products and ask respondents to rate their satisfaction with each item.

- Educational Quizzes: Add diagrams or pictures related to the quiz topics. For example, in a biology quiz, include images of plants or animals and ask students to identify them.

- Event Registrations: Use images of event speakers, venues, or past events to make the registration form more visually appealing.

2.2.2.2 Videos

Why Use Videos in Forms?

Videos can be an even more powerful tool than images when it comes to engaging your audience. They can provide dynamic content that explains complex topics, demonstrates processes, or adds a personal touch to your form. For example, in a training assessment, a video can be used to present a scenario, followed by questions that test the viewer's understanding. In surveys, videos can be used to show product demonstrations, advertisements, or other relevant content before asking for feedback.

Adding Videos to Your Questions

Adding a video to a Microsoft Form is straightforward and can be done in a few steps:

1. Select the Question: Choose the question where you want to include the video.

2. Click on the Video Icon: In the question editor, click on the video icon, which resembles a small play button.

3. Choose the Video Source: Microsoft Forms allows you to add videos primarily from YouTube. This integration makes it easy to embed YouTube videos directly into your form.

- YouTube URL: Simply copy the URL of the desired YouTube video and paste it into the provided field.

- Search YouTube: You can also search for a video directly within the Microsoft Forms interface by typing keywords related to the content you want to include.

4. Position the Video: Once the video is added, you can adjust its position within the question. It can be placed before the question text or after it, depending on what makes the most sense for your content flow.

5. Add a Caption or Description: If needed, you can add a caption or brief description under the video. This is useful for providing context or instructions related to the video content.

Best Practices for Using Videos

- Content Relevance: Ensure that the video content directly relates to the questions or the purpose of the form. For instance, a product demo video should be followed by questions about the product's features or user experience.

- Length and Engagement: Keep videos short and to the point. Long videos might lead to respondent fatigue, causing them to skip questions or abandon the form altogether. Ideally, videos should be less than two minutes.

- Mobile Optimization: Remember that many respondents may be viewing the form on a mobile device. Ensure that the video loads quickly and is viewable on smaller screens without issues.

- Interactivity: Consider using videos that encourage interaction or reflection. For example, a video that pauses at certain points and asks viewers to answer a question can increase engagement and retention.

Examples of Using Videos in Forms

- Training and Assessments: Embed a video that presents a case study or scenario, and then ask questions to assess understanding or gather feedback.

- Product Feedback: Use a product demo video to show a new feature, followed by questions asking for the respondent's opinion on it.

- Customer Satisfaction Surveys: Include a video message from the CEO or a company representative thanking customers for their feedback, making the survey feel more personal.

Combining Media with Text-Based Content

One of the strengths of Microsoft Forms is the ability to combine different types of content to create a rich and engaging experience for the user. By mixing text, images, and videos, you can cater to different learning styles and preferences, making your forms more accessible and effective.

Engagement and Clarity

The combination of text, images, and videos can help make your forms more engaging and easier to understand. For example, a complex question about a process can be broken down with a video demonstration, followed by text explanations and a related image. This approach not only makes the content clearer but also keeps the respondent engaged.

Interactive Learning

In educational contexts, combining different media types can create an interactive learning experience. A form could start with a brief introduction (text), followed by a tutorial (video), and end with a set of review questions (text and images). This multi-modal approach helps reinforce learning and keeps the participant engaged.

Enhancing Professional Presentations

For business or professional surveys, using a mix of media can elevate the quality of the form. For instance, a customer satisfaction survey can include a brief company introduction video, images of products or services, and well-crafted text questions. This not only collects valuable data but also reinforces the company's branding and messaging.

Conclusion

Adding media to your Microsoft Forms is a powerful way to enhance the user experience, making your forms more engaging, informative, and visually appealing. Whether you're using images to clarify a question or videos to provide additional context, these elements can help make your forms more effective and memorable. By following the steps and best practices outlined in this section, you can create forms that not only gather data efficiently but also leave a positive impression on respondents.

2.3 Setting Form Options

When creating a form, one of the key aspects to ensure a smooth and personalized experience for respondents is configuring the form options appropriately. These settings can significantly enhance the effectiveness of the form by tailoring it to different scenarios and needs. Two of the most crucial features under form options are Branching Logic and Response Settings. In this section, we will dive deep into Branching Logic, explaining its purpose, how to implement it, and best practices for using it effectively.

2.3.1 Branching Logic

Branching Logic, also known as conditional branching, is a powerful feature in Microsoft Forms that allows you to create a dynamic form experience. This feature lets you control the flow of your form based on the respondents' answers to previous questions. By using Branching Logic, you can guide users to relevant questions, skip unnecessary ones, or direct them to different sections of the form, creating a more personalized and efficient user experience.

What is Branching Logic?

Branching Logic allows you to set up rules that determine which question or section a respondent sees next based on their answer to a specific question. This means that respondents won't have to navigate through questions that are irrelevant to them, making the form completion process quicker and more user-friendly. For example, if you're creating a customer satisfaction survey and a respondent indicates that they are unhappy with a product, Branching Logic can direct them to a section where they can provide detailed feedback, while satisfied customers might skip this section entirely.

Benefits of Using Branching Logic

The primary benefit of using Branching Logic is the ability to streamline the respondent's experience. By presenting only the relevant questions, you can reduce the time it takes to complete the form and minimize respondent fatigue, which often leads to higher response rates and more accurate data. Additionally, Branching Logic can help in gathering more targeted and actionable insights by focusing the respondent's attention on specific areas of interest or concern.

Here are some of the key advantages of using Branching Logic in your forms:

- Personalization: Customize the respondent's journey through the form based on their answers, making the experience feel more tailored to their needs.

- Efficiency: Skip irrelevant questions, reducing the overall length of the form and making it easier for respondents to complete.

- Data Quality: By focusing on relevant questions, you are more likely to gather detailed and useful information, which can lead to better analysis and decision-making.

- Improved Response Rates: A shorter, more relevant form is less likely to be abandoned, leading to higher completion rates.

How to Implement Branching Logic

Implementing Branching Logic in Microsoft Forms is straightforward, but it requires careful planning to ensure that the logic flows correctly and that all possible respondent paths are covered. Below is a step-by-step guide on how to set up Branching Logic in your form.

Step 1: Plan Your Form Structure

Before you start implementing Branching Logic, it's important to plan out the structure of your form. Identify the questions that will trigger a branch and determine the possible paths respondents might take based on their answers. It's helpful to sketch out a flowchart or outline the form on paper before you start building it in Microsoft Forms. This will help you visualize the different paths and ensure that you don't miss any branches.

Step 2: Create Your Questions

Once you have a clear plan, start by creating all the questions in your form. Even if some questions are conditional and won't appear for every respondent, it's important to create them all before setting up the branching logic. This ensures that all possible paths are available for configuration.

Step 3: Set Up Branching Logic

To set up Branching Logic in Microsoft Forms:

1. Select the Question: Go to the question that will trigger the branch. This is typically a multiple-choice question or any other question type where the response can guide the next step.

2. Click on the 'More Options' (three dots) icon: Next to the question, click on the three dots to open a drop-down menu.

3. Choose 'Add Branching': From the drop-down menu, select 'Add Branching'. This will take you to a new interface where you can define the branching rules.

4. Define Branches: For each possible answer to the question, specify which question or section the respondent should be directed to next. You can direct respondents to a specific question, skip to a different section, or even end the form based on their response.

   - If you want a certain answer to lead to a specific follow-up question, select that question from the list.

   - If you want to skip questions, choose the question that respondents should jump to after selecting a particular answer.

   - To end the form after a specific answer, select the 'End of the Form' option.

5. Review and Save: Once you've set up the branching logic for a question, review the paths to ensure they align with your intended flow. After confirming that everything is correct, save your settings.

6. Test the Form: It's crucial to test the form before distributing it to ensure that the branching works as expected. Try answering the form in different ways to check that respondents are directed to the correct questions or sections based on their answers.

Step 4: Adjust and Refine

After testing, you might find areas where the branching logic needs adjustment. Perhaps a certain branch doesn't flow as smoothly as anticipated, or you might realize that additional branching is needed to handle more complex scenarios. Make any necessary adjustments and test again.

Best Practices for Using Branching Logic

To maximize the effectiveness of Branching Logic in your forms, consider the following best practices:

1. Keep It Simple: While it can be tempting to create complex branches, try to keep your logic as simple as possible. Overly complicated branching can confuse respondents or lead to errors in the form flow.

2. Test Thoroughly: Always test your form thoroughly before distributing it. Make sure that all branches work correctly and that respondents are guided through the form in the way you intend.

3. Provide Clear Instructions: If your form has multiple branches, it might be helpful to provide instructions at the beginning, so respondents understand that their answers will direct them to different parts of the form. This can reduce confusion and ensure a better response experience.

4. Use Branching to Enhance User Experience: Focus on using branching to enhance the user experience by reducing unnecessary questions and guiding respondents to relevant sections based on their answers. This not only improves response rates but also ensures that the data collected is more relevant and useful.

5. Review the Data: After collecting responses, review the data to ensure that the branching logic worked as intended. Look for patterns or anomalies that might indicate issues with the logic.

Examples of Effective Branching Logic

Example 1: Customer Feedback Form

In a customer feedback form, you might ask if the respondent is satisfied with a product. If they answer "No," you can branch them to a series of questions asking for more detailed feedback on what went wrong. If they answer "Yes," they might be directed to a different set of questions that focus on what they liked most about the product.

Example 2: Employee Engagement Survey

In an employee engagement survey, you could use branching to ask follow-up questions only to those who indicate that they are unhappy with certain aspects of their job. This way, you gather more in-depth insights from dissatisfied employees without burdening satisfied employees with unnecessary questions.

Example 3: Educational Assessment

In an educational assessment, you might ask students if they are confident in their understanding of a particular topic. Those who answer "No" can be directed to additional questions that assess where they might need further support, while those who answer "Yes" can skip ahead to the next topic.

Conclusion

Branching Logic is a crucial tool in Microsoft Forms that allows you to create dynamic, user-friendly forms that cater to the needs of each respondent. By carefully planning your form's structure and implementing branching logic effectively, you can enhance the overall user experience, improve data quality, and make your forms more efficient. Whether you're creating a simple survey or a complex questionnaire, understanding and utilizing Branching Logic will help you achieve better results and make your forms more effective.

2.3.2 Response Settings

When designing forms or surveys with Microsoft Forms, configuring the response settings is a crucial step that can significantly impact the effectiveness of your data collection and the overall user experience. Properly setting these options ensures that your form collects the right data in a manner that meets your objectives while respecting the privacy and preferences of your respondents. In this section, we will delve into the various response settings available in Microsoft Forms, exploring how to customize them to suit your needs.

2.3.2.1 Collecting Responses

One of the first decisions you'll need to make when setting up response settings is how you want to collect responses. Microsoft Forms offers several options, each tailored to different scenarios:

a. Anyone with the Link Can Respond:

This setting allows anyone with the form's link to fill it out. It's ideal for public surveys or forms where you don't need to track respondents' identities or restrict access. For instance, if you're conducting a customer satisfaction survey and want as many responses as possible, this setting is useful. However, because it's open to anyone with the link, there's no way to prevent multiple submissions from the same person unless you add specific restrictions or logic to the form.

b. Only People in My Organization Can Respond:

This option restricts form access to people within your organization who are logged in with their company email. This is particularly useful for internal surveys, feedback forms, or data collection where you need to ensure that only employees or authorized individuals can respond. Microsoft Forms will automatically capture the respondent's identity, so there's no need to ask for their name or email address. This also helps prevent duplicate submissions since each person can only submit one response unless you allow multiple responses (which we'll cover later).

c. Specific People in My Organization Can Respond:

This more restrictive setting allows only selected individuals or groups within your organization to access the form. You can specify these users or groups by entering their names or email addresses. This setting is perfect for confidential surveys, sensitive information collection, or targeted feedback where you need to control exactly who can submit responses. It ensures that only those who have been invited can participate.

d. One Response Per Person:

By default, Microsoft Forms allows only one response per person when "Only people in my organization" is selected. This setting is important if you want to ensure that each individual submits only one set of answers. It's particularly useful for official surveys, elections, or any scenario where multiple submissions could skew results. If this option is unchecked, respondents can submit the form multiple times, which might be necessary for forms like incident reports or other situations where an individual might need to report multiple entries.

2.3.2.2 Notification and Acknowledgment

Notification settings in Microsoft Forms can enhance both the respondent's experience and your ability to manage the responses efficiently.

a. Receive Email Notifications for Each Response:

Enabling this option allows the form owner to receive an email every time someone submits a response. This is particularly useful for forms that require immediate action or monitoring, such as job applications, incident reports, or urgent feedback forms. The email notification includes a summary of the response, making it easy to review and act upon the data quickly.

b. Send a Receipt to Respondents:

This option, available when collecting responses from people within your organization, sends a confirmation email to the respondent once they submit the form. The receipt includes a copy of their responses, which is beneficial for transparency and record-keeping. This is particularly useful in scenarios where respondents might need to reference their submissions later, such as for order confirmations, application forms, or any situation where the respondent needs proof of submission.

c. Customize the Thank You Message:

After a respondent submits the form, they are shown a thank you message. This message can be customized to provide additional information, express gratitude, or give further instructions. For example, you might want to inform respondents that their feedback will be reviewed and that they will hear back from you within a certain timeframe. Customizing the thank you message enhances the respondent's experience by making the interaction feel more personal and complete.

2.3.2.3 Data Privacy and Security

In today's world, data privacy and security are paramount. Microsoft Forms provides several settings that help ensure your data collection adheres to best practices in these areas.

a. Data Encryption:

All data collected via Microsoft Forms is encrypted, both in transit and at rest, ensuring that your respondents' information is secure. While this is managed automatically by Microsoft, it's essential to communicate to respondents that their data is being handled securely. This can be done by including a brief privacy notice at the beginning of your form or in the thank you message, explaining how their data will be used and protected.

b. Anonymous Responses:

If you want to collect data without capturing respondents' identities, you can set your form to allow anonymous responses. This is especially important for sensitive surveys where respondents might be reluctant to share honest feedback if they believe their responses could be traced back to them. Anonymous responses encourage honesty and openness, particularly in areas like employee satisfaction surveys, whistleblower reports, or other sensitive feedback mechanisms.

c. Compliance with Data Regulations:

Depending on your location and the nature of your survey, you might need to ensure that your data collection complies with specific regulations like GDPR (General Data Protection Regulation) in Europe or HIPAA (Health Insurance Portability and Accountability Act) in the United States. Microsoft Forms is designed to help you meet these requirements, but it's essential to review your form settings and ensure they align with the relevant laws and guidelines. This might include getting explicit consent from respondents, ensuring data is stored in specific regions, or implementing additional security measures.

2.3.2.4 Managing Response Limits and Deadlines

To control the flow of responses and ensure that your data collection is timely and manageable, Microsoft Forms provides options for setting response limits and deadlines.

a. Setting a Response Deadline:

You can set a specific date and time after which the form will no longer accept responses. This is useful for time-sensitive surveys, event registrations, or any scenario where you need to collect data within a specific period. Once the deadline passes, anyone attempting to submit the form will see a message indicating that the form is no longer accepting responses.

b. Limiting the Number of Responses:

In some cases, you might need to limit the number of responses your form can accept. This is particularly useful for event registrations where space is limited, or for promotions and offers where only a certain number of participants can benefit. Once the limit is reached, the form will automatically stop accepting responses, preventing oversubscription and helping you manage capacity effectively.

c. Pausing or Closing the Form Manually:

Even without a set deadline or response limit, you might need to close your form manually. Microsoft Forms allows you to pause or close the form at any time. This can be useful if circumstances change or if you've received enough data and want to stop further submissions. You can easily reopen the form later if needed.

2.3.2.5 Analyzing and Exporting Response Data

Once you've collected your responses, analyzing and exporting the data is the next crucial step. Microsoft Forms offers several tools to help you make sense of the data you've gathered.

a. Real-Time Response Visualization:

As responses come in, Microsoft Forms automatically generates charts and summaries to help you visualize the data in real-time. These visualizations are particularly helpful for spotting trends or outliers quickly. You can view summary statistics for each question, including the distribution of answers, average ratings, and more.

b. Exporting to Excel:

For more in-depth analysis, you can export your response data to Excel. This allows you to manipulate the data, create custom reports, or conduct advanced statistical analysis. Exporting to Excel is simple, and the exported file includes all the responses in a structured format, ready for further analysis. This is particularly useful for large surveys where the built-in Microsoft Forms analytics might not be sufficient.

c. Sharing Results with Stakeholders:

Microsoft Forms allows you to share the results with others, either by giving them access to the form's response summary or by sharing the exported data. You can control who has access to the results, ensuring that sensitive data is only shared with those who need to see it. This feature is particularly useful for team projects, where multiple people need to review and discuss the results.

d. Using Power BI for Advanced Analytics:

For even more powerful data analysis, you can integrate your form data with Power BI. Power BI allows you to create detailed dashboards, combine data from multiple sources, and generate insights that are not easily accessible through standard tools. This integration is ideal for organizations that rely on data-driven decision-making and need to extract maximum value from their survey results.

2.3.2.6 Customizing Response Experiences

To enhance the respondent's experience, you can customize various aspects of the form's response process, making it more engaging and aligned with your brand or communication style.

a. Redirecting Respondents After Submission:

After respondents submit their form, you can redirect them to a specific webpage. This is useful for guiding them to additional resources, thanking them in a more personalized manner, or leading them to a next step in a multi-part process. For example, after completing a survey, respondents could be redirected to a page that offers related content, a download link, or further instructions.

b. Customizing Error Messages:

Sometimes, respondents might encounter issues while filling out the form, such as not completing required fields or entering invalid data. Microsoft Forms allows you to customize the error messages that appear, making them more user-friendly or specific to the context of your form. This reduces frustration and helps ensure that the data you collect is accurate and complete.

c. Branding Your Form:

While Microsoft Forms offers basic customization options,

 you can take it a step further by ensuring that the entire experience reflects your brand. This can include customizing the thank you message, redirect page, and even the domain name used for the form link (if using advanced features through Microsoft 365). A consistent brand experience can enhance trust and make the form feel more integrated with your organization's other communications.

2.3.2.7 Ethical Considerations in Data Collection

Lastly, it's important to consider the ethical implications of your data collection practices. Ensuring that your form respects respondents' rights and fosters trust is essential for any organization.

a. Informed Consent:

Before collecting any data, it's crucial to obtain informed consent from respondents. This means clearly explaining what data you're collecting, how it will be used, and who will have access to it. Providing this information upfront and requiring respondents to acknowledge it before submitting the form helps ensure transparency and trust.

b. Anonymity vs. Confidentiality:

Decide whether your form will be anonymous or confidential, and communicate this clearly to respondents. In anonymous forms, no identifiable information is collected, while in confidential forms, such information might be collected but is kept private and secure. Understanding the difference and applying the appropriate settings is crucial depending on the nature of your survey.

c. Data Retention and Deletion Policies:

Consider how long you will retain the data collected through your form and what your deletion policies will be. It's important to have a clear data retention policy that complies with legal requirements and respects respondents' privacy. Additionally, giving respondents the option to withdraw their data or request its deletion can further enhance trust and ethical compliance.

In summary, configuring the response settings in Microsoft Forms is a comprehensive process that involves careful consideration of how you collect, manage, and utilize respondent data. By thoughtfully setting up these options, you can ensure that your forms are not only effective in gathering the information you need but also respectful of the rights and preferences of your respondents.

CHAPTER III
Customizing Your Form

3.1 Theme and Appearance

Customizing the visual appearance of your form is an essential aspect of creating an engaging and professional-looking survey or quiz. Microsoft Forms provides a range of tools to help you tailor the theme and appearance to align with your branding or simply to make your form more visually appealing. In this chapter, we'll explore how to apply and customize themes effectively.

3.1.1 Applying Themes

When creating a form, one of the easiest ways to enhance its visual appeal is by applying a theme. Microsoft Forms offers a variety of pre-built themes that you can apply with just a few clicks. These themes come with preset color schemes, background images, and fonts, providing a quick and easy way to give your form a polished look.

Understanding the Importance of Themes

Before diving into how to apply a theme, it's crucial to understand why themes matter. A well-chosen theme can do more than just make your form look good—it can also enhance user engagement and convey the tone of your survey or quiz. For example, a formal, corporate theme may be suitable for business-related forms, while a bright and colorful theme might be better for educational quizzes or feedback forms.

A theme can also help ensure consistency across all the forms you create, particularly if you are using Microsoft Forms in a business or educational setting. Consistent themes reinforce brand identity and make it easier for respondents to recognize and engage with your content.

Selecting a Theme

To begin applying a theme to your form, follow these steps:

1. Open Your Form: Start by opening the form you want to customize in Microsoft Forms.

2. Access the Theme Menu: Click on the "Theme" button located in the top-right corner of the form editor. This will open the theme menu, displaying various theme options.

3. Browse Available Themes: Scroll through the available themes. You will see a selection of options that include different color schemes, background images, and font styles. Each theme provides a preview of how it will look when applied to your form.

4. Apply a Theme: Once you find a theme that suits your needs, click on it to apply it to your form. The changes will be applied immediately, and you can see how the theme affects the overall appearance of your form.

Customizing a Pre-Built Theme

While the pre-built themes in Microsoft Forms offer a good starting point, you may want to further customize the theme to better match your specific needs. Here's how you can tweak a theme:

1. Change the Background Image:

   - If the default background image of the theme doesn't suit your form, you can replace it with one of your own. To do this, click on the "Background Image" icon within the theme menu. You can upload an image from your computer or select one from the available stock images provided by Microsoft.

   - When choosing a background image, consider its relevance to the form content and its impact on readability. For instance, a simple, muted image works well as it does not distract from the form's text.

2. Adjusting Colors:

   - You can also customize the color scheme of the theme. Click on the "Color" option within the theme menu to access the color picker. You can choose from a predefined set of colors or create a custom color by entering a hex code or using the color wheel.

- When selecting colors, it's important to consider color contrast to ensure that the text is legible against the background. High-contrast color combinations, such as dark text on a light background, generally offer better readability.

3. Font Customization:

- While Microsoft Forms does not provide extensive font customization options like some other tools, you can still influence the look of the text through the theme. Each theme comes with its own set of fonts that will be applied to your form. If the font style is critical to your branding, choose a theme that aligns closely with your desired font aesthetics.

- Ensure that the font used is easy to read and matches the tone of your form. For example, a serif font might be more appropriate for formal or academic surveys, while a sans-serif font could be better suited for casual or modern forms.

Using Custom Themes for Branding

For organizations that require a consistent branding across all forms, Microsoft Forms allows you to create and use custom themes. This feature is particularly useful for businesses, educational institutions, and other organizations where maintaining a consistent brand image is important.

1. Creating a Custom Theme:

- While Microsoft Forms does not currently support the creation of fully custom themes within the interface, you can achieve a branded look by consistently applying your organization's colors, fonts, and background images across all forms.

- Create a template form that includes your preferred theme settings. You can then duplicate this form whenever you need to create a new one, ensuring consistency in appearance.

2. Applying a Consistent Brand Identity:

- If your organization uses a specific set of colors or a logo, incorporate these elements into your forms. Use the custom color feature to match your brand's color scheme, and consider using a background image that features your company's logo or other branding elements.

- Consistent branding helps to establish trust and recognition with respondents. When your audience sees the same branding across multiple forms, they are more likely to engage, knowing that the content is coming from a trusted source.

Best Practices for Theme Application

While themes can greatly enhance the appearance of your form, it's essential to apply them thoughtfully. Here are some best practices to consider:

1. Prioritize Readability:

- No matter how attractive a theme may look, it should not compromise the readability of your form. Avoid overly complex backgrounds that can make text hard to read. Stick to high-contrast color schemes where the text is clearly visible against the background.

2. Match the Theme to the Content:

- The theme should reflect the purpose of the form. For instance, a fun, colorful theme might be appropriate for a quiz aimed at students, while a more subdued, professional theme would be better for a business survey.

3. Test on Different Devices:

- Ensure that your form looks good on various devices, including desktops, tablets, and smartphones. A theme that looks great on a large screen might not translate well to a smaller one, so testing across devices is crucial.

4. Keep it Simple:

- Sometimes, less is more. A simple, clean theme is often more effective than one that is overly elaborate. The focus should always be on the content of the form, not just the design.

5. Consider Accessibility:

- Make sure that your chosen theme supports accessibility features. This includes ensuring that color contrast is sufficient for those with visual impairments and that the form is navigable using keyboard shortcuts and screen readers.

Summary of Applying Themes

Applying a theme to your form in Microsoft Forms is a straightforward process that can significantly enhance the user experience. Whether you choose a pre-built theme or customize one to fit your specific needs, the theme plays a critical role in the form's visual appeal and overall effectiveness.

By following the steps outlined above and considering best practices, you can create forms that not only look great but also function effectively for your intended audience. Themes should be chosen with care, ensuring that they align with the form's purpose and content while also maintaining readability and accessibility.

In the next section, we will explore more advanced customization options, including how to modify specific question types to better engage respondents and capture more accurate data.

3.1.2 Customizing Colors and Fonts

Customizing the colors and fonts of your Microsoft Forms is an essential step in creating a form that not only meets your functional needs but also reflects your brand or personal style. The appearance of your form can greatly influence how respondents perceive it, which in turn can impact response rates and data quality. In this section, we'll explore the various ways to customize the colors and fonts of your forms, providing detailed instructions and best practices to ensure your form is visually appealing and effective.

3.1.2.1 Understanding the Impact of Colors and Fonts

Before diving into the technical steps of customization, it's important to understand the psychological impact that colors and fonts can have on your respondents. Colors can evoke emotions and set the tone of your form. For example:

- Blue is often associated with trust and professionalism, making it a good choice for business-related forms.

- Green is linked to growth, tranquility, and health, which can be ideal for environmental or health-related surveys.

- Red can signify urgency or importance but can also be overwhelming if overused.

Similarly, fonts can affect readability and the perceived seriousness of your form. A well-chosen font can enhance readability and ensure that your form is taken seriously. Conversely, an inappropriate font might make your form look unprofessional or difficult to read, deterring respondents.

3.1.2.2 Applying Custom Colors

Microsoft Forms provides several built-in themes that you can apply with a single click, but for those looking to tailor their form's appearance to match a specific brand or aesthetic, customizing colors is a more flexible option.

Step-by-Step Guide to Customizing Colors:

1. Accessing the Theme Panel:

   - After opening your form in Microsoft Forms, click on the Theme button at the top right of the interface. This will open the theme panel where you can see various preset themes.

2. Choosing a Base Theme:

   - You can start by selecting a base theme that closely aligns with your desired color scheme. Even if you plan to customize further, choosing a relevant base theme can save time and serve as a good starting point.

3. Customizing the Background Color:

   - To change the background color, click on the Custom Theme option in the theme panel.

   - Here, you can input a specific hex color code if you have a precise color in mind. If not, you can use the color picker to find the exact shade you want.

   - Once selected, the background of your form will change to reflect this new color.

4. Adjusting Form Color Accents:

   - In addition to the background, you can also customize the accent colors used for buttons, links, and other interactive elements.

   - In the same Custom Theme section, look for options to adjust these colors. This ensures that your entire form is cohesive and aligned with your brand's color palette.

5. Previewing the Form:

   - After making your color selections, it's a good idea to preview your form to see how it looks from a respondent's perspective. Click on the Preview button at the top right of the screen.

   - Ensure that the colors look good on different devices (e.g., desktop, tablet, mobile) and that they do not impede readability.

Best Practices:

- Contrast: Ensure there is enough contrast between the text and background to make the form easy to read. For instance, avoid light-colored text on a light background.

- Consistency: Stick to a limited color palette to maintain consistency and avoid overwhelming your respondents.

- Brand Alignment: If the form is for an organization, ensure the colors align with your company's branding guidelines.

3.1.2.3 Selecting and Customizing Fonts

Fonts are just as critical as colors in creating an aesthetically pleasing and functional form. Microsoft Forms provides a range of fonts that you can choose from, but selecting the right one requires some thought.

Step-by-Step Guide to Customizing Fonts:

1. Accessing Font Options:

   - Within the same Theme panel, after customizing colors, you will find options to change the font of your form.

2. Choosing a Font:

   - Microsoft Forms typically offers a selection of standard fonts. These may include classic options like Arial, Times New Roman, and modern fonts like Segoe UI or Calibri.

- Select a font that matches the tone of your survey. For formal business surveys, a clean and professional font like Arial or Calibri is ideal. For more creative or informal surveys, you might choose something more stylized.

3. Customizing Font Size:

- While Microsoft Forms does not currently allow for extensive customization of font sizes for different sections, it generally uses a readable font size across all devices.

- You can, however, ensure that the chosen font is readable by testing the form across different devices.

4. Applying Font Customizations:

- Once you've selected the desired font, it will automatically apply to all text in your form, including questions, answers, and any descriptive text.

5. Testing Readability:

- As with colors, it's crucial to preview the form to ensure that the font is easily readable. Test it on different devices and in different lighting conditions to ensure the text remains clear and legible.

Best Practices:

- Readability: Choose a font that is easy to read. Avoid overly decorative fonts that may reduce readability, especially for longer surveys.

- Consistency: Use the same font throughout the form to maintain a consistent look and feel.

- Device Compatibility: Test your form on various devices to ensure the font renders well on all screen sizes.

3.1.2.4 Combining Colors and Fonts for Maximum Impact

The real magic happens when you combine your custom colors and fonts in a way that enhances the overall user experience. Here are a few tips to ensure that your combination of colors and fonts is both visually appealing and effective:

- Harmonize Colors and Fonts: Ensure that the colors and fonts complement each other. For example, a modern, sans-serif font like Arial or Segoe UI pairs well with bright, bold colors, while a more traditional serif font like Times New Roman might work better with more muted, classic colors.

- Use Color to Highlight: Use accent colors to draw attention to important parts of your form, such as the submit button or critical instructions. However, be careful not to overdo it; too many highlights can reduce their effectiveness.

- Maintain Focus: Your customization should enhance the form's readability and user experience, not detract from it. Avoid using too many different fonts or colors, as this can make the form look cluttered and confusing.

3.1.2.5 Practical Examples of Effective Customization

To provide a clearer understanding of how these principles can be applied, let's consider a few practical examples:

Example 1: Corporate Survey

- Colors: Dark blue background with white text. Accent color in light blue for buttons and links.

- Font: Arial or Calibri for a clean, professional look.

- Impact: This color scheme and font combination create a professional and trustworthy appearance, ideal for internal company surveys or client feedback forms.

Example 2: Educational Quiz

- Colors: Light green background with dark green text. Use yellow as an accent color for questions and answers.

- Font: Segoe UI for a modern and approachable feel.

- Impact: The green tones evoke feelings of growth and learning, making it perfect for an educational setting, while the modern font keeps it fresh and engaging.

Example 3: Event Registration Form

- Colors: White background with dark purple text. Use gold as an accent color for headers and buttons.

- Font: Times New Roman or Georgia for a formal and elegant appearance.

- Impact: This combination gives the form a sophisticated look, suitable for formal events like weddings, galas, or corporate conferences.

3.1.2.6 Final Tips for Customization

To wrap up, here are some final tips to help you make the most out of your color and font customizations:

- Iterate: Don't be afraid to experiment with different color and font combinations. Create multiple versions of your form and test them with a small audience to gather feedback.

- Keep Accessibility in Mind: Always consider how your color and font choices will affect all users, including those with visual impairments. Use high contrast and clear, readable fonts to ensure your form is accessible to everyone.

- Stay Updated: Microsoft Forms periodically updates its features. Stay informed about any new customization options that may be released, as these could provide new opportunities to enhance your forms.

By thoughtfully customizing the colors and fonts of your Microsoft Forms, you can create forms that are not only functional but also visually engaging and aligned with your brand or purpose. This attention to detail can lead to higher response rates, better data quality, and a more positive experience for your respondents.

3.2 Advanced Question Options

3.2.1 Using Likert Scales

The Likert scale is a widely used tool in survey design that allows respondents to express their level of agreement or disagreement with a particular statement. In Microsoft Forms, incorporating Likert scales can significantly enhance the quality of data collected, as it enables a more nuanced understanding of respondents' attitudes and perceptions. This section will guide you through the process of creating, customizing, and effectively utilizing Likert scales in Microsoft Forms.

Understanding Likert Scales

Before diving into the technical aspects of using Likert scales in Microsoft Forms, it's important to understand what a Likert scale is and why it is useful. A Likert scale typically consists of a statement followed by a range of response options that reflect varying degrees of agreement, such as "Strongly Disagree," "Disagree," "Neutral," "Agree," and "Strongly Agree."

These scales are particularly useful for measuring attitudes, opinions, or behaviors because they provide a spectrum of responses, offering more insight than a simple yes/no question. By capturing degrees of sentiment, Likert scales allow for more detailed data analysis and interpretation.

Creating Likert Scales in Microsoft Forms

Microsoft Forms makes it easy to add Likert scales to your surveys or quizzes. Here's a step-by-step guide:

1. Start by Adding a New Question:

  - Open your form or quiz in Microsoft Forms.

  - Click on the Add New button to insert a new question.

  - Select the Likert option from the list of question types. This will automatically insert a Likert scale question template into your form.

2. Define Your Statements:

- Once the Likert scale question type is added, you'll see fields where you can enter your statements. These statements should be clear and concise, focusing on a single idea or concept to avoid confusion.

  - For example, if you're evaluating customer satisfaction, your statements might include:

    - "The product meets my expectations."

    - "Customer service was helpful and responsive."

    - "I would recommend this product to others."

3. Customize the Response Options:

- Below the statements, you can define the response options. Microsoft Forms typically provides default options like "Strongly Disagree," "Disagree," "Neutral," "Agree," and "Strongly Agree," but these can be customized to suit your needs.

- To customize, simply click on the response option text and edit it. For instance, if you're assessing frequency rather than agreement, you might use options like "Never," "Rarely," "Sometimes," "Often," and "Always."

4. Adjust the Number of Response Options:

- Microsoft Forms allows you to add or remove response options as needed. If you feel a five-point scale is too restrictive, you can easily add more options, such as "Somewhat Agree" or "Moderately Agree," to create a seven-point scale.

- Conversely, if simplicity is key, you can reduce the scale to three points, such as "Disagree," "Neutral," and "Agree."

5. Preview and Test:

- After setting up your Likert scale, it's important to preview your form to ensure that the scale looks correct and functions as intended.

- To do this, click on the Preview button at the top of the form editor. This will show you how the Likert scale will appear to respondents.

- Test the form by selecting different responses to make sure the scale is user-friendly and captures the data you need.

Best Practices for Designing Likert Scales

While creating Likert scales in Microsoft Forms is straightforward, designing effective scales that yield reliable data requires careful consideration. Here are some best practices to keep in mind:

1. Be Consistent with Response Options:

- Maintain consistency in the wording and order of your response options throughout your form. This helps respondents understand the scale and provides more reliable data.

- For example, if you start with "Strongly Disagree" on the left and "Strongly Agree" on the right, keep this order for all Likert scales in your form.

2. Balance the Scale:

- Ensure that your scale is balanced, with an equal number of positive and negative response options. This avoids biasing respondents toward a particular side of the scale.

- If you're using a five-point scale, a balanced setup would include two negative options, one neutral option, and two positive options.

3. Avoid Ambiguous Statements:

- Each statement on your Likert scale should be specific and unambiguous. Avoid double-barreled statements that combine two different ideas, as this can confuse respondents and lead to inaccurate data.

- For example, instead of saying, "The product is affordable and reliable," split it into two separate statements: "The product is affordable" and "The product is reliable."

4. Use Neutral Options Sparingly:

- While it's important to offer a neutral option, be mindful of its potential impact. If too many respondents select "Neutral," it may indicate that the statement is unclear or irrelevant. Consider revising the statement or exploring why respondents may not have strong opinions.

5. Consider the Length of the Scale:

- A typical Likert scale ranges from five to seven points. A five-point scale is usually sufficient for most surveys, providing enough variation without overwhelming respondents. However, if your topic is particularly nuanced, a seven-point scale might be more appropriate.

- Avoid scales that are too long (e.g., nine or more points), as this can lead to respondent fatigue and less reliable data.

Analyzing Data from Likert Scales

Once you've collected responses from your Likert scale, the next step is data analysis. Microsoft Forms provides several ways to analyze the data you've collected:

1. View Responses in Microsoft Forms:

- The Responses tab in Microsoft Forms gives you a quick overview of how respondents answered each question, including Likert scales. You'll see a summary of responses, usually displayed as a bar chart, showing the distribution of answers across the scale.

- This can give you an immediate sense of trends, such as whether most respondents agree or disagree with a particular statement.

2. Exporting Data to Excel:

- For more detailed analysis, you can export your survey data to Excel. This is particularly useful for Likert scales, as Excel allows you to calculate averages, medians, and other statistical measures.

- To export, simply click on the Open in Excel button in the Responses tab. Once in Excel, you can use formulas to quantify the responses. For example, you might assign numerical values to each response option (e.g., 1 for "Strongly Disagree" to 5 for "Strongly Agree") and calculate the average score for each statement.

3. Creating Visual Representations:

- Excel also enables you to create more sophisticated visualizations, such as pie charts, histograms, or scatter plots, to better understand your data. These can be particularly useful when presenting your findings to stakeholders.

4. Comparing Groups:

- If your survey includes demographic questions or other variables, you can segment your Likert scale data to compare responses between different groups. For example, you might compare satisfaction levels between different age groups or departments.

- This type of analysis can reveal deeper insights and help you tailor your actions based on specific group needs.

Applications of Likert Scales

Likert scales are versatile tools that can be used in a variety of contexts. Here are some common applications:

1. Customer Satisfaction Surveys:

- Likert scales are ideal for measuring customer satisfaction, where they can assess various aspects such as product quality, customer service, and overall experience.

- Example: "How satisfied are you with our customer service?" with options ranging from "Very Dissatisfied" to "Very Satisfied."

2. Employee Engagement Surveys:

- Use Likert scales to gauge employee satisfaction, engagement, and morale within your organization.

- Example: "I feel valued at work," with responses from "Strongly Disagree" to "Strongly Agree."

3. Educational Assessments:

- In educational settings, Likert scales can be used to evaluate student or teacher attitudes, learning outcomes, and course effectiveness.

- Example: "The course materials were clear and easy to understand," with options from "Strongly Disagree" to "Strongly Agree."

4. Market Research:

- Companies often use Likert scales in market research to understand consumer preferences, brand perception, and purchasing behavior.

- Example: "I prefer this brand over its competitors," with response options ranging from "Strongly Disagree" to "Strongly Agree."

Common Pitfalls and How to Avoid Them

While Likert scales are powerful tools, there are some common pitfalls to be aware of:

1. Scale Length Confusion:

- Sometimes, respondents may find it difficult to differentiate between adjacent options on a long scale (e.g., "Slightly Agree" vs. "Somewhat Agree"). To avoid this, keep your scale simple and ensure each option is clearly defined.

2. Central Tendency Bias:

- Respondents may gravitate toward the middle of the scale, particularly if they are unsure of their opinion or want to avoid extreme responses. This can skew your data towards neutrality.

- To mitigate this, ensure your statements are clear and relevant, and consider the context in which respondents are answering.

3. Overuse of Likert Scales:

- While Likert scales are useful, overloading your survey with them can lead to respondent fatigue, reducing the quality of your data. Balance your survey with other question types, such as open-ended questions or multiple-choice.

Conclusion

Likert scales are a powerful feature in Microsoft Forms that allow you to gather detailed, nuanced feedback from your respondents. By understanding how to create and use these scales effectively, you can improve the quality of the data you collect and gain deeper insights into your audience's attitudes and behaviors. Whether you're conducting customer satisfaction surveys, employee engagement assessments, or academic research, mastering Likert scales will enhance your survey's effectiveness and the actionable insights you derive from it.

3.2.2 Net Promoter Score (NPS) Questions

Net Promoter Score (NPS) is a widely recognized metric that helps organizations gauge customer loyalty by measuring their willingness to recommend a company's product or service to others. In this section, we'll delve into how you can effectively use NPS questions in Microsoft Forms, including the theory behind NPS, the setup process, best practices for interpretation, and strategies for leveraging the results to drive business improvements.

Understanding the Net Promoter Score (NPS) Concept

Before diving into the technical aspects of setting up NPS questions in Microsoft Forms, it is essential to understand the concept of NPS and why it is valuable. NPS is calculated based on responses to a single question:

> "On a scale from 0 to 10, how likely are you to recommend our company/product/service to a friend or colleague?"

Respondents are then categorized into three groups based on their score:

- Promoters (9-10): These are loyal enthusiasts who will likely refer others, fueling growth.

- Passives (7-8): Satisfied but unenthusiastic customers who are vulnerable to competitive offerings.

- Detractors (0-6): Unhappy customers who can damage your brand through negative word-of-mouth.

The NPS is then calculated by subtracting the percentage of Detractors from the percentage of Promoters. The score can range from -100 to +100, with higher scores indicating better customer loyalty.

Setting Up NPS Questions in Microsoft Forms

Microsoft Forms makes it easy to create and include NPS questions in your surveys. Here's a step-by-step guide to setting up an NPS question:

1. Adding an NPS Question:

   - Navigate to your form: Start by opening the form where you want to include the NPS question.

   - Add a new question: Click on the "Add Question" button. From the available question types, select "Likert" or a "Choice" question, depending on the layout you prefer.

   - Configure the question: Enter the standard NPS question: "On a scale from 0 to 10, how likely are you to recommend our company/product/service to a friend or colleague?".

   - Set the response scale: For a Likert question, you would create options labeled from 0 to 10. If using a Choice question, input the numbers 0 through 10 as individual options.

2. Customizing the NPS Question:

   - Optional sub-questions: You can add follow-up questions asking respondents to explain their score, which provides qualitative insights into their rating.

   - Branching logic: Use branching to direct Promoters, Passives, and Detractors to different follow-up questions, allowing you to gather more targeted feedback based on their response.

3. Styling and Layout:

   - Visual appeal: Customize the appearance of your NPS question to match your form's theme. Ensure the colors and fonts are consistent with your brand's identity to create a cohesive experience.

   - Accessibility considerations: Ensure that your NPS question is accessible to all respondents by using clear labels and providing any necessary descriptions or instructions.

Best Practices for Using NPS Questions

To get the most value out of NPS questions in your forms, it's important to follow certain best practices. Here's how you can ensure your NPS data is reliable, actionable, and drives meaningful improvements:

1. Position the NPS Question Strategically:

 - Early placement: Position the NPS question at the beginning of the survey to capture the respondent's initial sentiment. This is particularly useful if the survey is long, as respondents' opinions might shift after answering multiple questions.

 - Isolated question: Consider making the NPS question a standalone survey if you need a quick pulse on customer sentiment without additional context.

2. Accompanying Open-Ended Questions:

 - Follow-up with a "Why" question: Always follow the NPS question with an open-ended question asking respondents to explain their score. This provides context to the numeric score, helping you understand the reasons behind their satisfaction or dissatisfaction.

 - Avoid overloading: While additional questions can provide deeper insights, avoid adding too many follow-up questions that might lead to respondent fatigue.

3. Frequency and Timing of NPS Surveys:

 - Regular intervals: Conduct NPS surveys regularly (e.g., quarterly) to track changes in customer sentiment over time. This allows you to measure the impact of any changes or improvements you've implemented.

 - Key touchpoints: Send NPS surveys after key customer interactions, such as after a purchase, following customer support interactions, or after a product upgrade, to capture real-time feedback.

4. Analyzing and Interpreting NPS Data:

- Segmentation: Analyze NPS scores by segmenting the data based on customer demographics, purchase history, or other relevant criteria. This can reveal insights about specific groups, such as high-value customers or new users.

- Trend analysis: Look at NPS trends over time to identify patterns. Are scores improving after implementing certain changes? Are there seasonal dips that coincide with product launches or service disruptions?

Leveraging NPS Results for Business Improvement

Once you've collected and analyzed your NPS data, the next step is to use these insights to drive tangible improvements within your organization. Here's how you can make the most of your NPS results:

1. Acting on Feedback:

- Promoters: Engage with Promoters by encouraging them to leave reviews, refer others, or participate in case studies. Reward their loyalty with exclusive offers or recognition.

- Passives: Reach out to Passives with targeted offers or incentives to move them into the Promoter category. Identify common themes in their feedback to address any lingering concerns.

- Detractors: Prioritize resolving issues raised by Detractors. Implement service recovery strategies and follow up with these customers to demonstrate that their feedback is valued and acted upon.

2. Continuous Improvement:

- Feedback loops: Establish a closed-loop feedback system where teams are regularly reviewing NPS data and making iterative improvements. Ensure that changes based on feedback are communicated back to customers, reinforcing their importance.

- Cross-functional collaboration: Share NPS insights across different departments—such as product development, customer service, and marketing—to ensure a unified approach to addressing customer concerns and enhancing satisfaction.

3. Benchmarking and Goal Setting:

- Internal benchmarking: Compare your NPS over time or across different product lines, services, or locations to identify areas of strength and those needing improvement.

- External benchmarking: Compare your NPS with industry standards or competitors to understand your relative position in the market. This can guide strategic decisions and set realistic goals for improvement.

4. Reporting and Communicating NPS Results:

- Dashboards and reports: Use Microsoft Forms' integration with Power BI or Excel to create dashboards that visualize NPS trends and insights. This helps in sharing results with stakeholders in a clear and impactful way.

- Sharing results with teams: Regularly communicate NPS scores and feedback to teams across the organization. Recognize and celebrate improvements while addressing areas that need attention.

5. Using NPS as a Leading Indicator:

- Predicting future behavior: High NPS scores are often correlated with customer retention, repeat purchases, and positive word-of-mouth. Use NPS as a leading indicator to forecast business performance and customer loyalty.

- Incorporating NPS into KPIs: Consider integrating NPS into your organization's key performance indicators (KPIs). Tracking NPS alongside financial metrics and other business KPIs provides a more holistic view of your company's health.

Common Challenges and Solutions in NPS Implementation

While NPS is a powerful tool, organizations may face challenges when implementing and interpreting NPS surveys. Here are some common issues and strategies to overcome them:

1. Low Response Rates:

- Simplifying the process: Keep your NPS survey short and to the point. Clearly communicate the purpose of the survey and how the feedback will be used to encourage participation.

- Incentivizing responses: Offer small rewards or enter respondents into a raffle as an incentive to complete the survey.

2. Bias in Responses:

- Minimizing bias: Ensure that the survey is anonymous to encourage honest feedback. Avoid leading questions or language that might influence the respondent's rating.

- Balanced sampling: Ensure that your survey reaches a representative sample of your customer base, including both satisfied and dissatisfied customers.

3. Overemphasis on the NPS Score:

- Looking beyond the score: While the NPS number is important, it's crucial to focus on the qualitative feedback provided by respondents. The score alone won't provide the insights needed to drive meaningful change.

- Contextual analysis: Consider external factors such as market conditions, competitive actions, or recent product changes that might influence NPS scores.

4. Integrating NPS with Other Metrics:

- Holistic approach: Use NPS in conjunction with other customer satisfaction metrics, such as Customer Satisfaction Score (CSAT) or Customer Effort Score (CES), to gain a more comprehensive understanding of customer sentiment.

- Aligning with business goals: Ensure that NPS insights are aligned with your broader business objectives, such as improving customer retention, increasing lifetime value, or enhancing brand perception.

Conclusion

Net Promoter Score (NPS) questions in Microsoft Forms offer a powerful way to measure customer loyalty and gather actionable feedback. By setting up NPS questions effectively, adhering to best practices, and using the insights to drive continuous improvement, organizations can significantly enhance their customer experience and build long-term loyalty. As you incorporate NPS into your surveys, remember that the true value of NPS lies not just in the score itself, but in the actionable insights and improvements it can inspire.

3.3 Accessibility Features

3.3.1 Enabling Accessibility

In the realm of digital forms, accessibility is a fundamental aspect that ensures all users, including those with disabilities, can effectively interact with and benefit from the content provided. Microsoft Forms is designed with a focus on inclusivity, offering a range of features and settings to support users with varying needs. This section delves into how you can enable and enhance accessibility within your Microsoft Forms, ensuring your surveys and quizzes are accessible to a diverse audience.

1. Understanding Accessibility in Microsoft Forms

Accessibility in Microsoft Forms involves designing forms that can be used by everyone, including individuals with visual, auditory, motor, or cognitive impairments. This encompasses several practices, such as providing text alternatives for non-text content, ensuring keyboard navigability, and using clear and straightforward language. Microsoft Forms adheres to these principles to ensure inclusivity.

2. Key Accessibility Features in Microsoft Forms

Microsoft Forms incorporates several built-in features that help enhance accessibility:

- Alt Text for Images: When adding images to your forms, Microsoft Forms allows you to provide alternative (alt) text. This text is crucial for screen readers used by visually impaired users. It describes the content of the image so that users who cannot see it can still understand its purpose or meaning.

- Keyboard Navigation: Forms are designed to be navigable using a keyboard alone, which is essential for users who cannot use a mouse. Ensure that all interactive elements, such as questions, answer options, and buttons, can be accessed and operated via keyboard shortcuts.

- Color Contrast: Microsoft Forms ensures that the default color schemes adhere to accessibility standards, providing sufficient contrast between text and background colors. This is important for users with color vision deficiencies or low vision.

3. Enabling Accessibility Features in Microsoft Forms

To enable and enhance accessibility in your forms, follow these steps:

3.3.1.1 Adding Alt Text to Images

1. Insert an Image: Begin by adding an image to your form through the "Insert" option. You can upload an image file or choose from existing files in your OneDrive or library.

2. Add Alt Text: Once the image is inserted, click on the image to select it. You will see an option to add alt text. Click on this option to open the alt text editor.

3. Describe the Image: Enter a concise and descriptive text that conveys the content and purpose of the image. Avoid using vague descriptions like "image" or "picture"; instead, provide information about what the image depicts or its role in the form.

4. Save and Review: After adding the alt text, save your changes and review the form to ensure that the text accurately represents the image. This helps users relying on screen readers to understand the context and content of your images.

3.3.1.2 Ensuring Keyboard Navigation

1. Test Navigation: Use the tab key to navigate through the different fields and interactive elements in your form. Ensure that each element is accessible and can be selected using keyboard shortcuts.

2. Focus Indicators: Check that focus indicators (such as outlines or highlights) are visible around interactive elements. These indicators help users who rely on keyboard navigation to identify the currently selected field or button.

3. Accessible Form Elements: Ensure that all form elements, including questions, answer options, and buttons, are properly labeled and can be accessed using keyboard commands. This includes checking that dropdowns, radio buttons, and checkboxes are functional and navigable.

4. Keyboard Shortcuts: Familiarize yourself with keyboard shortcuts for Microsoft Forms to assist users who navigate forms without a mouse. Providing a list of available shortcuts can be helpful for users with motor impairments.

3.3.1.3 Color Contrast and Text Readability

1. Select Accessible Colors: Choose form themes and color schemes that offer high contrast between text and background colors. This helps users with color vision deficiencies and those with low vision to read and interact with the form content easily.

2. Test Color Combinations: Use online tools or accessibility checkers to test color contrast ratios. These tools can help you determine if the color combinations meet accessibility standards and are readable for users with different types of visual impairments.

3. Provide Text Alternatives: For any text-based content, ensure that the font size and style are legible. Avoid using overly decorative fonts that may be difficult to read, and ensure that the text size is large enough to be easily readable.

4. Best Practices for Accessible Form Design

4.1 Clear and Concise Language

1. Use Simple Language: Write questions and instructions in clear, straightforward language. Avoid jargon or complex terminology that might be difficult for users with cognitive impairments to understand.

2. Provide Instructions: Include clear instructions for each section or question in the form. This helps users understand what is expected and reduces confusion.

4.2 Logical Structure and Flow

1. Organize Content: Arrange questions and content in a logical order. Group related questions together and use sections or headings to break up the form into manageable parts.

2. Use Branching Logic: Implement branching logic to show or hide questions based on previous answers. This creates a more tailored experience and prevents users from encountering irrelevant or confusing questions.

4.3 Testing and Feedback

1. Conduct Usability Testing: Before finalizing your form, conduct usability testing with individuals who have disabilities. This helps identify potential accessibility issues and allows you to make necessary adjustments.

2. Seek Feedback: Encourage feedback from users regarding the accessibility of your form. This feedback can provide valuable insights into areas that may need improvement and help you create more inclusive forms.

5. Conclusion

Enabling and enhancing accessibility in Microsoft Forms is a crucial aspect of creating inclusive surveys and quizzes. By utilizing the built-in features and following best practices, you can ensure that your forms are accessible to all users, regardless of their abilities. This not only adheres to accessibility standards but also demonstrates a commitment to inclusivity, making your forms more effective and user-friendly for a diverse audience.

3.3.2 Tips for Accessible Form Design

Ensuring that your forms are accessible is crucial for inclusivity and effectiveness. Accessible forms enable all users, regardless of their abilities or disabilities, to complete and submit them successfully. This section will provide comprehensive tips for designing accessible forms using Microsoft Forms.

1. Understanding Accessibility Standards

Before diving into the specifics, it's important to understand what accessibility means in the context of form design. Accessibility standards, such as the Web Content Accessibility Guidelines (WCAG) and Section 508 of the Rehabilitation Act, offer guidelines on how to make content accessible to people with disabilities. Familiarizing yourself with these standards will help you design forms that comply with legal requirements and best practices.

Key Accessibility Guidelines

- WCAG Principles: The four principles of WCAG are Perceivable, Operable, Understandable, and Robust (POUR). Each principle addresses different aspects of accessibility.

- Section 508: This U.S. law requires federal agencies to make their electronic and information technology accessible to people with disabilities.

2. Designing for Screen Readers

Screen readers are software programs used by individuals with visual impairments to read digital content aloud. Designing your form to be compatible with screen readers involves several key practices:

2.1 Use Descriptive Labels and Instructions

- Labels: Ensure each form field has a clear and descriptive label. For example, instead of "Name," use "Full Name" to provide additional context.

- Instructions: Include brief, clear instructions for each section of the form. These instructions should be visible to users who rely on screen readers.

2.2 Provide Alternative Text for Media

- Images: Include alternative text (alt text) for any images or graphics used in the form. Alt text should describe the content and function of the image.

- Videos: If you include videos, provide captions and transcripts to make the content accessible to users who are deaf or hard of hearing.

2.3 Use ARIA Roles and Landmarks

- ARIA Roles: Accessible Rich Internet Applications (ARIA) roles help describe the purpose of elements on the page. For example, use `role="button"` for interactive elements that act as buttons.

- Landmarks: ARIA landmarks (e.g., `role="main"`, `role="navigation"`) help users navigate the form more easily by identifying different sections.

3. Designing for Keyboard Navigation

Many users rely on keyboards or keyboard-like devices to navigate forms. Ensuring that your form is keyboard-friendly involves the following practices:

3.1 Ensure Logical Tab Order

- Tab Order: Arrange the tab order of form fields logically so users can navigate through the form in a predictable sequence. Users should be able to tab through the fields without confusion.

3.2 Provide Visible Focus Indicators

- Focus Indicators: Ensure that when a form field is selected, it is visually distinct from the rest of the content. This helps users understand where they are within the form.

3.3 Include Keyboard Shortcuts

- Shortcuts: If your form includes buttons or actions that can be triggered by keyboard shortcuts, clearly indicate these options. This can enhance the experience for keyboard users.

4. Designing for Cognitive Accessibility

Cognitive accessibility focuses on making content understandable and usable for individuals with cognitive disabilities. Here are some tips for designing forms with cognitive accessibility in mind:

4.1 Use Simple Language and Instructions

- Language: Use clear and straightforward language. Avoid jargon and complex terms that might confuse users.

- Instructions: Provide step-by-step instructions to guide users through the form.

4.2 Organize Content Clearly

- Logical Grouping: Group related fields together and use headings or sections to separate different parts of the form.

- Consistent Layout: Maintain a consistent layout throughout the form to avoid confusing users.

4.3 Provide Help and Error Messages

- Help Text: Include help text or tooltips that offer additional guidance on completing form fields.

- Error Messages: Ensure error messages are clear and provide specific instructions on how to correct mistakes.

5. Testing Your Form for Accessibility

Testing is a critical step in ensuring your form is accessible. Here's how you can test your form to identify and address potential accessibility issues:

5.1 Use Accessibility Testing Tools

- Automated Tools: Tools like WAVE, Axe, and Lighthouse can scan your form for common accessibility issues and provide recommendations for improvement.

- Manual Testing: Complement automated tests with manual testing to ensure that all aspects of accessibility are covered.

5.2 Conduct User Testing with People with Disabilities

- User Feedback: Engage individuals with disabilities to test your form and provide feedback on their experience. This can help identify areas for improvement that automated tools might miss.

5.3 Review and Update Regularly

- Ongoing Review: Regularly review and update your form to ensure continued compliance with accessibility standards and address any new issues that arise.

6. Implementing Accessibility Features in Microsoft Forms

Microsoft Forms offers various features to help you create accessible forms. Here's how to use these features effectively:

6.1 Using Built-In Accessibility Options

- Accessibility Checker: Use Microsoft Forms' built-in accessibility checker to identify and address accessibility issues.

- Form Design Tools: Utilize Microsoft Forms' design tools to create forms that are easy to navigate and understand.

6.2 Customizing Accessibility Settings

- Custom Styles: Apply custom styles that improve readability and contrast, especially for users with visual impairments.

- Feedback Options: Customize feedback options to ensure they are accessible and provide clear instructions for users.

7. Conclusion

Designing accessible forms is not just a legal requirement but a commitment to inclusivity and user experience. By following the tips outlined in this section, you can create forms that are usable and effective for everyone, regardless of their abilities or disabilities. Accessibility should be a fundamental consideration in all aspects of form design, ensuring that your forms serve all users effectively and equitably.

CHAPTER IV
Managing Form Responses

4.1 Collecting Responses

One of the most crucial steps after creating a form is collecting responses. Microsoft Forms provides a robust and flexible set of tools that allow you to distribute your form to respondents in various ways. Understanding how to effectively collect responses is essential to ensuring that your survey or quiz reaches the intended audience and generates the data you need.

The process of collecting responses begins with sharing your form. Microsoft Forms makes this process simple and accessible, whether you're distributing the form to a small, targeted group or a broad audience across different platforms. In this section, we'll explore various methods of sharing your form, including sharing via a direct link, email, and embedding the form on a website. We'll also discuss response options that allow you to control who can respond and how they can do so.

4.1.1 Sharing Your Form

Sharing your form is a critical step in the data collection process. Microsoft Forms offers multiple ways to share your form with respondents, each with its advantages depending on your audience and the purpose of your survey or quiz. Below are the primary methods of sharing a form in Microsoft Forms:

Via Link

Sharing your form via a link is one of the most straightforward methods available. This approach is versatile and can be used across various platforms, such as email, social media, or messaging apps. Here's how you can share your form using a link:

Creating a Shareable Link:

- Once your form is complete, click on the "Share" button located at the top right corner of the Microsoft Forms interface.

- A window will pop up with different sharing options. By default, the first option presented is a shareable link.

- Microsoft Forms allows you to customize the type of link you generate based on who you want to respond. For example, you can create a link that allows anyone with the link to respond, or restrict it to specific people within your organization.

Types of Links:

- Anyone with the Link: This option is ideal when you want to distribute the form widely without restricting access. This link can be shared publicly, and anyone who clicks on it will be able to fill out the form. However, keep in mind that this option might reduce control over who responds, and it may lead to duplicate or irrelevant responses.

- People in My Organization: If your form is intended only for colleagues within your organization, this option ensures that only those with a company account can access the form. This helps in maintaining privacy and ensuring that responses are relevant.

- Specific People: For highly targeted forms, you can specify the email addresses of the individuals who are allowed to respond. This option is useful when dealing with confidential information or when you need to ensure that only selected people provide input.

Sharing the Link:

- After choosing the appropriate link type, click on "Copy" to copy the link to your clipboard.

- You can now paste this link into an email, a chat, or any other platform where you want to share the form. The link can also be shortened for easier sharing if you plan to distribute it via social media or SMS.

Best Practices for Sharing via Link:

- Shorten Your Link: If you plan to share your form on platforms like Twitter or SMS, where character limits are a concern, use a URL shortener to make the link more manageable.

- Accompany with Instructions: When sharing the link, especially via email or social media, include a brief description or instructions. This helps respondents understand the purpose of the form and what is expected from them.

- Monitor Link Sharing: If you notice an unusually high number of responses or responses from unexpected sources, consider adjusting your form settings to restrict access.

Advantages of Sharing via Link:

- Simplicity: The process of generating and sharing a link is quick and easy.

- Versatility: Links can be shared across multiple platforms and mediums.

- Broad Reach: This method allows you to reach a wide audience, making it ideal for public surveys or quizzes.

Considerations:

- Security Concerns: Links shared publicly can be accessed by anyone, which may lead to unwanted or irrelevant responses. Consider using the "People in My Organization" or "Specific People" options to mitigate this risk.

- Response Monitoring: It's essential to monitor responses to ensure the data collected is from your intended audience. Microsoft Forms provides tools for tracking and analyzing responses to help with this.

Via Email

Sharing your form via email is another effective way to distribute it, especially when you have a specific list of recipients in mind. Email allows you to directly reach your audience and often yields higher response rates due to the personalized nature of the communication.

Steps to Share via Email:

- In the Microsoft Forms interface, after clicking the "Share" button, select the "Email" option.

- You can enter the email addresses of your recipients directly into the provided field. Microsoft Forms allows you to send the form to multiple recipients at once.

- If you use Outlook, you can integrate directly with it to access your contacts and send the form. The form will appear as a link within the email body.

- You can customize the email by adding a subject line and a personalized message that explains the purpose of the form and encourages recipients to participate.

Advantages of Sharing via Email:

- Direct Reach: Email allows you to target specific individuals or groups, ensuring that the form reaches the intended audience.

- Personalization: You can customize the message to make it more relevant and appealing to the recipients, which can increase response rates.

- Tracking: Email platforms often allow you to track whether recipients have opened the email and clicked on the form link, providing insights into engagement.

Best Practices for Email Sharing:

- Craft a Compelling Subject Line: The subject line should be clear and concise, encouraging recipients to open the email and complete the form.

- Clear Call-to-Action: Ensure that the email content includes a strong call-to-action that directs recipients to click on the link and fill out the form.

- Follow-Up: If response rates are low, consider sending a follow-up email as a reminder. Microsoft Forms does not natively support this, but you can manage follow-ups manually or through your email client.

Considerations:

- Email Deliverability: Ensure that your emails are not flagged as spam. Personalizing the email content and avoiding excessive links or attachments can help with this.

- Recipient Privacy: Be mindful of privacy laws and ensure that you have the recipients' consent to send them emails, especially if they are external contacts.

Embedding on a Website

Embedding your form on a website is an excellent way to collect responses directly from visitors. This method is particularly useful for organizations, businesses, or educators who want to integrate the form seamlessly into their web presence.

Steps to Embed a Form:

- After clicking the "Share" button in Microsoft Forms, choose the "Embed" option.

- Microsoft Forms will generate an HTML code snippet that you can copy.

- Paste this code into the HTML of your website where you want the form to appear. The form will be embedded directly on the page, allowing visitors to fill it out without leaving the site.

Customization Options:

- Adjusting the Embed Code: You can customize the embed code to adjust the size of the form, ensuring it fits well within your webpage layout.

- Inline Embedding: Embed the form directly within the content of a blog post, article, or landing page to make it a natural part of the visitor's experience.

- Popup Forms: If you prefer, you can embed the form as a popup that appears when visitors click a button or link. This approach is less intrusive and can be used for surveys, feedback forms, or newsletter sign-ups.

Advantages of Embedding:

- Seamless Integration: The form is part of your website, making it easier for visitors to respond without navigating away from the page.

- Professional Presentation: Embedding a form on your site can enhance the professionalism and user experience, especially if it's well-designed and aligned with your website's theme.

- Increased Visibility: Forms embedded on high-traffic pages are more likely to attract responses, especially if the form's purpose aligns with the content on the page.

Best Practices for Embedding:

- Responsive Design: Ensure that the form is responsive and works well on different devices, including smartphones and tablets.

- Prominent Placement: Place the form in a visible and accessible area of the webpage to maximize responses.

- Clear Instructions: Provide context or instructions around the form, so visitors understand what the form is for and why they should complete it.

Considerations:

- Website Performance: Ensure that embedding the form does not slow down your website or disrupt the user experience. Testing the form on various devices and browsers can help identify and fix any issues.

- Brand Consistency: Customize the form's appearance to match your website's branding, ensuring a consistent look and feel across your site.

4.1.2 Response Options

Microsoft Forms offers several response options to cater to different data collection needs. Understanding and configuring these options effectively can greatly enhance the quality and usability of the data you collect. This section explores the various response options available in Microsoft Forms, including response settings, restrictions, and customization features that allow you to tailor your form to meet specific objectives.

Setting Response Collection Parameters

When designing a form or quiz, one of the first decisions you'll make is how to configure the response collection parameters. These settings determine who can respond to your form, how many responses each participant can submit, and how long the form will be open for submissions.

a. Who Can Respond?

Microsoft Forms provides flexibility in choosing who can respond to your form. You can limit responses to specific individuals or groups, or you can open the form to anyone with the link.

- Anyone with the Link: This option allows anyone who has the form link to respond, regardless of whether they are inside or outside your organization. It's ideal for public surveys, feedback forms, or quizzes that require a wide audience.

- People in My Organization: This option restricts responses to individuals who are part of your organization. It's useful for internal surveys, quizzes, or feedback forms where you only want input from employees or specific teams.

- Specific People in My Organization: If you need even more control, you can specify which individuals or groups within your organization can respond. This is particularly useful for targeted feedback or when you need responses from a specific department or team.

b. Allowing Multiple Responses

Depending on the purpose of your form, you may want to allow or restrict multiple responses from the same participant.

- One Response per Person: This setting ensures that each respondent can only submit one response. It's useful for forms where you need to ensure unique data entries, such as in official surveys or exams.

- Multiple Responses: Allowing multiple responses from the same person can be beneficial in scenarios like feedback forms where participants might need to submit feedback on different topics or at different times.

c. Start and End Dates

You can set specific start and end dates for your form to control when it is available for responses.

- Start Date: Setting a start date ensures that the form is only available from a particular date and time. This is useful if you're planning to launch the form as part of a campaign or event.

- End Date: The end date closes the form automatically after a certain date and time, ensuring no further responses are collected. This is essential for time-sensitive surveys or quizzes.

Response Restrictions

Microsoft Forms allows you to apply various restrictions on the responses, ensuring that the data collected meets your specific needs. These restrictions can be applied to individual questions or to the form as a whole.

a. Requiring Responses

You can make specific questions mandatory by marking them as required. This ensures that respondents cannot submit the form without answering those questions, which is crucial for gathering complete data.

- Required Questions: Marking a question as required forces respondents to provide an answer before moving to the next question or submitting the form. This is useful for critical information that you need from every respondent.

- Optional Questions: Leaving questions optional gives respondents the freedom to skip questions that may not be relevant to them, making the form more flexible and less overwhelming.

b. Limiting Response Options

You can restrict the type and range of responses to ensure data accuracy.

- Response Validation: For questions requiring numerical, text, or date inputs, you can set validation rules to control the type of data entered. For example, you can restrict a text field to only accept email addresses, or a numerical field to only accept values within a certain range.

- Character Limits: For text responses, you can set a character limit to control the length of the answer. This is useful when you need concise answers, such as in summary or short-answer questions.

c. Response Frequency and Timing

Managing how frequently respondents can submit their responses can prevent data skewing.

- Time Limits on Quizzes: If you're using Microsoft Forms for quizzes, you can set time limits for each section or the entire quiz. This feature is essential for assessing how quickly respondents can answer the questions, adding an element of challenge and time management.

- Throttling Responses: In scenarios where you expect high traffic, you can throttle responses to prevent server overload. While this is generally handled by Microsoft's backend, being aware of potential limitations helps in planning large-scale surveys.

Customizing Response Settings

Beyond basic restrictions, Microsoft Forms allows you to customize response settings to better align with your data collection goals.

a. Notifications and Acknowledgements

Acknowledging receipt of responses is a good practice, especially in surveys or forms that involve external stakeholders or customers.

- Send Receipt to Respondents: You can enable a setting that sends a receipt to respondents after they complete the form. This is particularly useful in formal surveys or feedback forms where participants expect confirmation of their submission.

- Custom Thank You Message: After submitting a form, respondents can be redirected to a custom thank you page. This message can include next steps, additional resources, or simply an appreciation note. It helps enhance the participant's experience and encourages future engagement.

b. Anonymity Settings

Ensuring respondent anonymity can encourage more honest and open responses, especially in sensitive surveys or feedback forms.

- Anonymous Responses: You can choose to make responses anonymous, meaning that no personal identifiers (like email addresses) will be collected. This setting is crucial for surveys dealing with sensitive topics where privacy is a concern.

- Collecting Identifiable Information: Conversely, if you need to follow up with respondents or link responses to specific individuals, you can choose to collect identifying information such as names or email addresses. This setting is common in employee feedback forms, quizzes, or assessments.

c. Custom Response Limits

Setting custom response limits allows you to control the volume of data collected.

- Limiting Total Responses: If you're conducting research or running a promotional event with a limited number of slots, you can cap the number of responses your form will accept. Once the limit is reached, the form will automatically close, preventing any further submissions.

- First-Come, First-Served Basis: For events or offers with limited availability, you can design your form to accept responses on a first-come, first-served basis. This creates urgency and encourages prompt responses.

Using Response Data for Further Actions

After configuring response settings, it's essential to think about how the data will be used post-collection. Microsoft Forms integrates well with other Microsoft 365 apps, allowing you to automate processes based on form responses.

a. Automating Workflows with Power Automate

Power Automate allows you to create workflows that trigger actions based on form submissions.

- Automatic Email Notifications: Set up a workflow that sends an email notification to a specific team member or department when a form is submitted. This is useful for alerting relevant stakeholders in real-time, such as in customer service feedback or lead generation forms.

- Data Export and Backup: Automate the process of exporting form data to Excel or other databases. This ensures that all responses are backed up and available for analysis without manual intervention.

b. Integrating with Microsoft Teams

For organizations that use Microsoft Teams, integrating Microsoft Forms can streamline team collaboration and response management.

- Posting Responses in Teams Channels: Automatically post form responses in a Teams channel for immediate review and discussion. This integration is particularly useful in team environments where quick decision-making is required based on form data.

- Creating Tasks from Responses: Convert form responses into tasks in Microsoft Planner or other task management tools within Teams. This feature helps in converting survey or feedback data into actionable tasks, enhancing productivity.

c. Utilizing Responses in SharePoint

If your organization uses SharePoint, form responses can be directly integrated into SharePoint lists or libraries for further processing and documentation.

- Storing Responses in SharePoint Lists: Automatically store form responses in a SharePoint list, where they can be further categorized, filtered, and used in conjunction with other SharePoint features.

- Document Generation: Use form responses to automatically generate documents in SharePoint, such as certificates, reports, or contracts. This automation saves time and ensures consistency in document creation.

Conclusion

Microsoft Forms offers a wide array of response options that cater to different survey and quiz needs. By understanding and effectively configuring these options, you can ensure that your form collects the most relevant and accurate data possible. From restricting responses to automating workflows, the tools provided by Microsoft Forms not only enhance the data collection process but also streamline the subsequent data management and analysis tasks. Proper use of these response settings can significantly increase the efficiency and effectiveness of your surveys and quizzes, ultimately leading to better decision-making and insights.

4.2 Viewing and Analyzing Responses

Once you've successfully collected responses for your Microsoft Forms survey or quiz, the next crucial step is to view and analyze the data. This process is essential for understanding trends, gathering insights, and making informed decisions based on the feedback received. Microsoft Forms offers a variety of tools to help you navigate through your data efficiently, enabling you to see the bigger picture or dive deep into individual responses.

4.2.1 Response Summary

The Response Summary in Microsoft Forms is a powerful feature that gives you an immediate overview of how respondents answered your survey or quiz. This feature is designed to simplify the process of analyzing your data, providing you with visual representations and statistics that can help you quickly grasp the overall results.

Overview of the Response Summary

When you navigate to the "Responses" tab in Microsoft Forms, you are immediately presented with the Response Summary. This section displays aggregated data for each question in your form, offering a snapshot of your respondents' answers. The data is typically presented in the form of charts, graphs, and statistics, which are automatically generated by Microsoft Forms based on the type of question and the nature of the responses.

Visualizing the Data

1. Pie Charts:

 - Pie charts are commonly used for multiple-choice questions, where each slice of the pie represents the percentage of respondents who selected a particular answer. This visual tool is particularly effective for quickly identifying the most popular choices among your respondents. For instance, if you asked a question about preferred products, the pie chart would visually show which product is the most favored.

2. Bar Charts:

- Bar charts are another frequently used visualization tool in the Response Summary. These are ideal for questions with multiple options, such as Likert scales or rating questions. Each bar represents the number of respondents who selected each option, allowing you to see at a glance how opinions or preferences are distributed. This is particularly useful for questions that involve rating satisfaction levels, where you can easily compare the frequency of responses across different satisfaction categories.

3. Aggregated Statistics:

- For questions that involve numerical data, such as rating scales or numerical inputs, Microsoft Forms provides aggregated statistics including averages, minimum and maximum values, and standard deviations. These statistics are invaluable for understanding the central tendencies and variations in your data. For example, if you conducted a satisfaction survey with a rating scale from 1 to 10, the average rating would give you a clear indication of overall satisfaction levels.

4. Text Responses:

- For open-ended questions, the Response Summary presents a list of all text responses. While these are not visualized in charts, Microsoft Forms allows you to read through each response individually or look for common themes and keywords. This type of qualitative data can provide deep insights into the specific thoughts and opinions of your respondents, offering context that quantitative data might not reveal.

Interpreting the Summary Data

Interpreting the data in the Response Summary involves more than just looking at the numbers; it's about understanding what those numbers mean for your specific context. Here are some key considerations when interpreting your summary data:

1. Identifying Trends:

- Look for patterns in the data that indicate trends. For example, if a majority of respondents are selecting a particular option consistently, this could indicate a strong preference or consensus among your audience. In contrast, a wide distribution of answers might suggest varied opinions or uncertainty among respondents.

2. Spotting Outliers:

- Outliers can be just as informative as trends. If a particular response is significantly more or less popular than others, it might be worth investigating why. Outliers could indicate areas where your audience has strong feelings, either positively or negatively, or they could highlight issues with how a question was framed.

3. Comparing Against Expectations:

- Compare the summary data against your expectations or previous data. Are the responses in line with what you anticipated, or are there surprises? Discrepancies between expectations and actual responses can be a valuable indicator of shifting opinions or unmet needs.

4. Assessing Response Distribution:

- Consider how evenly distributed the responses are. For example, in a satisfaction survey, if most respondents rate their satisfaction as either very high or very low with few in the middle, this might suggest polarization within your audience. On the other hand, a more balanced distribution might indicate a generally moderate level of satisfaction.

5. Understanding Context:

- Always interpret your data in the context of your specific survey or quiz goals. For instance, if the purpose of your form was to gather feedback on a new product, high ratings in the summary might indicate a successful launch, whereas low ratings could suggest areas that need improvement.

Using the Response Summary for Decision-Making

The Response Summary isn't just a tool for viewing data—it's a resource for making informed decisions. Here's how you can leverage the summary data to drive action:

1. Identifying Areas of Improvement:

- Use the Response Summary to pinpoint areas that need attention. For instance, if feedback indicates dissatisfaction with a particular aspect of a service or product, you can prioritize improvements in that area. The visual data makes it easier to identify which aspects are most in need of change.

2. Celebrating Successes:

- Positive feedback can be just as valuable. Use the data to recognize areas where you're doing well. High ratings or positive trends can inform your team about what's working, providing a basis for reinforcing successful strategies.

3. Tailoring Future Surveys:

- The insights gained from the Response Summary can also inform the design of future surveys. For example, if you notice that certain types of questions yielded more insightful responses, you might choose to include similar questions in future surveys to gather even more valuable data.

4. Reporting to Stakeholders:

- The clear and concise visualizations provided in the Response Summary are ideal for reporting to stakeholders. Whether you're presenting to management, team members, or external partners, the summarized data can effectively communicate the key findings from your survey or quiz.

Customizing the Response Summary

While Microsoft Forms provides a robust set of default visualizations, you might find that customizing the way data is displayed better suits your needs:

1. Filtering Responses:

- Microsoft Forms allows you to filter responses based on various criteria, such as date range or specific answers. This can be particularly useful if you're looking to analyze responses from a specific subset of your audience. For instance, if you conducted a survey over several weeks, filtering responses by week can help you understand how opinions evolved over time.

2. Customizing Charts:

- Although Microsoft Forms automatically generates charts based on your data, you can often adjust the chart type to better suit your needs. For example, you might prefer a bar chart over a pie chart for certain data sets, or you might want to adjust the scale of a graph to better reflect the distribution of responses.

3. Adjusting Data Display:

- In some cases, you may want to adjust how data is displayed to highlight specific insights. For example, if you're only interested in responses that meet a certain threshold (e.g., ratings above 8 out of 10), you can focus the summary on those data points, providing a clearer view of high-performing areas.

Exporting the Response Summary

Microsoft Forms also offers the ability to export your response summary data for use in other applications:

1. Exporting to Excel:

- One of the most common ways to work with your data outside of Microsoft Forms is to export it to Excel. This allows for more advanced data analysis, including the use of pivot tables, complex formulas, and custom charts. Excel provides a robust environment for digging deeper into your data, allowing you to perform sophisticated analysis that might not be possible directly within Microsoft Forms.

2. Integrating with Power BI:

- For more advanced data visualization and reporting, consider integrating your data with Power BI. This tool allows you to create interactive dashboards and reports that can be shared with stakeholders. Power BI can take the insights from your Response Summary and elevate them into dynamic visualizations that can be updated in real-time.

3. Sharing Summary Data:

- If you need to share the summary data with others who don't have access to Microsoft Forms, you can export the visualizations and statistics as images or PDFs. This allows you to include them in presentations, reports, or emails, ensuring that your insights are easily accessible to all relevant parties.

Conclusion

The Response Summary feature in Microsoft Forms is an essential tool for anyone looking to effectively manage and analyze survey or quiz data. By providing immediate, visual feedback on how respondents answered your questions, it allows you to quickly gain insights and make informed decisions. Whether you're looking to improve a product, gather feedback on a service, or simply understand your audience better, the Response

Summary gives you the tools you need to interpret your data and take action based on your findings. As you continue to use Microsoft Forms, becoming proficient in leveraging the Response Summary will significantly enhance your ability to collect and utilize feedback effectively.

4.2.2 Individual Responses

When using Microsoft Forms for data collection, one of the most powerful features is the ability to view and analyze individual responses. This functionality allows users to dive deeply into each participant's submission, providing insights that are crucial for detailed analysis, personalized feedback, and decision-making processes.

Accessing Individual Responses

To begin exploring individual responses, navigate to the "Responses" tab of your form. Here, you'll find a summary of all collected data, including the number of responses, average time taken to complete the form, and other aggregated statistics. To view individual responses, click on the "View results" button or select "Review answers."

Microsoft Forms presents individual responses in a straightforward, user-friendly interface. Each response is displayed sequentially, showing the participant's answers exactly as they were submitted. You can use the navigation arrows or the drop-down menu to move through each response, allowing you to review them one by one. This detailed view helps you understand how each respondent interacted with the form and can provide context that aggregated data might overlook.

Analyzing Individual Responses

Analyzing individual responses is essential for identifying patterns, outliers, and specific feedback that may not be apparent when looking at summary data alone. Here's how you can approach this analysis:

1. Identifying Trends and Patterns

   - Qualitative Analysis: For open-ended questions, such as text responses, reviewing individual answers allows you to capture nuances in language, tone, and content. You can identify common themes or concerns that respondents may share. For instance, in a customer feedback form, consistent mentions of a specific issue across multiple responses can indicate a systemic problem that needs addressing.

- Quantitative Analysis: For closed-ended questions, such as multiple-choice or Likert scale questions, individual responses can reveal patterns in preferences or behaviors. For example, if several respondents select the same option consistently, it might indicate a strong consensus or a trend worth investigating further.

2. Identifying Outliers

- Outliers are responses that differ significantly from the majority. These can be particularly insightful in understanding edge cases or unique perspectives. For instance, in a satisfaction survey, if most respondents rate their experience highly, but one respondent gives a very low score, reviewing their individual response can provide clues about what went wrong in their case.

- Outliers can also highlight potential issues with the form itself, such as questions that might be confusing or misinterpreted by certain respondents. In such cases, examining the outlier responses closely can help you refine and improve your form for future use.

3. Providing Personalized Feedback

- If your form or quiz is designed to assess knowledge or gather information for a personalized response, viewing individual answers is crucial. For example, in an educational setting, reviewing individual quiz responses allows instructors to provide tailored feedback to students, addressing specific mistakes or misconceptions.

- Personalized feedback based on individual responses can also enhance user engagement and satisfaction. For instance, in a training program, recognizing and responding to individual progress can motivate participants and improve learning outcomes.

4. Cross-Referencing Responses

- Microsoft Forms allows you to cross-reference answers within an individual response, which can be particularly useful when analyzing complex surveys. For example, in a survey that includes demographic questions alongside opinion-based questions, you can analyze how respondents from different age groups or regions answered specific questions. This can provide deeper insights into how different segments of your audience think or behave.

Exporting Individual Responses for Further Analysis

While Microsoft Forms provides a robust platform for viewing and analyzing individual responses, exporting these responses to other tools, such as Excel, can offer even greater analytical capabilities. Here's how you can do this:

1. Exporting to Excel

- By exporting responses to Excel, you can create custom views, apply filters, and use Excel's advanced functions to analyze individual responses in more detail. For instance, you might use pivot tables to organize and summarize responses by category or use Excel's graphing tools to visualize trends across individual answers.

- Exporting also allows you to archive individual responses for long-term storage or for comparison with future data collections. This can be valuable in longitudinal studies or when tracking changes in opinions or behaviors over time.

2. Integrating with Other Applications

- Individual responses exported to Excel can be easily integrated with other Microsoft 365 tools, such as Power BI for advanced data visualization or Access for database management. This integration allows for more sophisticated data analysis, including multi-variable analysis, predictive modeling, and more.

- You can also use tools like Power Automate to automate the process of exporting and analyzing individual responses, saving time and ensuring consistency in your analysis workflows.

Practical Applications of Individual Response Analysis

Understanding how to view and analyze individual responses is critical in various scenarios. Here are some practical applications across different fields:

1. Education

- Student Assessments: Teachers can review individual quiz responses to assess student understanding and provide targeted feedback. For example, a teacher might analyze how each student answered specific questions to identify common areas of difficulty and adjust their teaching strategy accordingly.

- Course Evaluations: Educational institutions can use surveys to collect feedback from students about courses or instructors. By analyzing individual responses, administrators can identify specific concerns or areas for improvement that might not be apparent in aggregated data.

2. Customer Feedback

- Product Feedback: Companies often use forms to collect feedback on products or services. By reviewing individual responses, product managers can understand how different customers perceive specific features, identify common pain points, and prioritize enhancements.

- Support Experience: In customer support, analyzing individual responses to satisfaction surveys can help identify recurring issues or exceptional service cases. This allows support teams to address concerns proactively and improve overall customer experience.

3. Human Resources

- Employee Surveys: HR departments can use individual responses from employee surveys to gauge morale, job satisfaction, or the effectiveness of company policies. This detailed view helps HR professionals address specific issues raised by employees and tailor interventions to meet their needs.

- Recruitment Forms: During recruitment, reviewing individual candidate responses to application forms or pre-screening questionnaires allows recruiters to evaluate qualifications, fit for the role, and potential areas for follow-up during interviews.

4. Market Research

- Consumer Insights: Market researchers can use forms to gather insights from individual consumers. By analyzing individual responses, researchers can identify distinct consumer segments, preferences, and purchasing behaviors, which can inform product development and marketing strategies.

- Focus Groups: In focus group studies, individual responses can provide detailed insights into participant opinions, allowing researchers to understand the nuances of consumer attitudes and behaviors.

Ensuring Data Privacy and Ethical Considerations

When analyzing individual responses, it's important to consider data privacy and ethical implications. Microsoft Forms provides several tools and settings to help ensure compliance with data protection regulations and to respect the privacy of respondents:

1. Anonymizing Responses

- Depending on the nature of your form, you may choose to anonymize individual responses to protect the identity of participants. Microsoft Forms allows you to collect data without capturing identifiable information, which is especially important in sensitive surveys or research studies.

2. Data Security

- Ensure that individual responses are stored securely and that access is restricted to authorized personnel only. Microsoft Forms integrates with the broader Microsoft 365 security framework, providing robust data protection measures, including encryption and compliance with industry standards.

3. Ethical Use of Data

- When reviewing individual responses, consider the ethical implications of how this data is used. Ensure that respondents are informed about how their data will be used and that their consent has been obtained where necessary. Avoid using data in ways that could harm or unfairly disadvantage participants.

Conclusion

Viewing and analyzing individual responses in Microsoft Forms is a critical component of effective data collection and analysis. By accessing and reviewing these responses, you gain valuable insights into the thoughts, preferences, and behaviors of your respondents. Whether you're using Microsoft Forms for education, customer feedback, HR, or market research, understanding how to navigate and interpret individual responses will enhance your ability to make informed decisions, provide personalized feedback, and ultimately achieve your goals.

As you continue to explore Microsoft Forms, remember that the power of individual response analysis lies not just in the data itself, but in the actions you take based on that data. Use the tools and techniques discussed in this section to harness the full potential of the responses you collect, driving meaningful improvements and achieving greater success in your surveys and quizzes.

4.3 Exporting and Using Data

4.3.1 Exporting to Excel

Exporting data to Excel from Microsoft Forms is a powerful feature that allows users to manipulate, analyze, and present data in a flexible and comprehensive manner. This functionality is essential for users who need to perform advanced data analysis, create detailed reports, or simply manage large amounts of response data more effectively.

Introduction to Exporting Data

When you conduct a survey or quiz using Microsoft Forms, the responses are automatically collected and stored in the cloud. While Microsoft Forms provides a basic interface for viewing and analyzing this data, exporting the data to Excel opens up a world of possibilities for more in-depth analysis. Excel is a versatile tool that offers a wide range of features for data manipulation, including sorting, filtering, creating pivot tables, and generating charts.

Exporting to Excel is particularly useful in scenarios where you need to:

- Perform complex data analysis beyond the capabilities of Microsoft Forms.

- Combine data from multiple forms or sources.

- Share data with colleagues or stakeholders who prefer or require data in Excel format.

- Create customized reports or dashboards.

Steps to Export Data to Excel

The process of exporting your form responses to Excel is straightforward. Below is a step-by-step guide to exporting data from Microsoft Forms to Excel:

1. Accessing Your Form's Responses:

  - Navigate to Microsoft Forms, and select the form you wish to export responses from.

- Click on the "Responses" tab at the top of the form. This will display a summary of the collected responses.

2. Exporting the Data:

- On the "Responses" tab, look for the "Open in Excel" button. This button is usually located at the top right corner of the response summary section.

- Click the "Open in Excel" button. This action will trigger the export process, and an Excel file containing all the response data will be downloaded to your device.

- Depending on your browser settings, you may be prompted to save the file or it may be automatically saved to your default download location.

3. Understanding the Exported Excel File:

- The exported Excel file will contain a table with all the responses. Each row represents a single response, while each column corresponds to a question in your form.

- The first column typically contains a unique identifier for each response, while subsequent columns contain the answers provided by respondents.

- If your form includes questions with multiple options (e.g., multiple-choice questions), each selected option will be displayed in the corresponding cell.

Working with the Exported Data in Excel

Once you have exported your data to Excel, you can leverage Excel's robust features to manage and analyze the data. Here are some of the key tasks you might perform:

1. Data Cleaning:

- Removing Duplicates: If your dataset contains duplicate responses, you can use Excel's "Remove Duplicates" feature to clean your data.

- Correcting Errors: Sometimes, manual input errors might occur, such as incorrect date formats or typographical errors. These can be corrected directly in Excel.

- Handling Missing Data: If some responses are incomplete, you can choose to filter out those rows or input estimated values where necessary.

2. Sorting and Filtering Data:

  - Sorting: You can sort your data alphabetically, numerically, or by date to organize your responses in a way that is meaningful for your analysis.

  - Filtering: Excel's filter feature allows you to display only the data that meets certain criteria. For example, you can filter responses to show only those from a specific date range or those that selected a particular answer option.

3. Analyzing Data with PivotTables:

  - Creating PivotTables: PivotTables are an incredibly powerful tool in Excel that allows you to summarize large datasets quickly. You can create a PivotTable to analyze your form responses by various categories, such as by respondent demographics or by the answers to specific questions.

  - Drilling Down Data: With PivotTables, you can drill down into specific data points to explore underlying details, providing deeper insights into your survey or quiz results.

4. Visualizing Data with Charts:

  - Creating Charts: Excel offers a variety of chart types, including bar charts, pie charts, line graphs, and more. You can use these charts to visualize your survey or quiz data, making it easier to communicate your findings to others.

  - Customizing Charts: Once you have created a chart, you can customize it by changing the colors, labels, and data series to better match your reporting needs.

5. Combining Data from Multiple Forms:

  - If you have conducted multiple surveys or quizzes and want to combine the results, Excel allows you to import data from different files and merge them into a single dataset. This is particularly useful for longitudinal studies or comparative analyses across different groups or time periods.

6. Using Formulas for Advanced Analysis:

  - Excel's formula capabilities are vast. You can use formulas to calculate averages, sums, percentages, or even more complex statistical measures such as standard deviation or correlation.

  - Conditional Formatting: This feature allows you to apply formatting to cells based on certain conditions, such as highlighting all responses that scored below a certain threshold.

Practical Examples of Exported Data Use

To better understand how exporting data to Excel can be utilized, here are some practical examples:

1. Educational Quizzes:

- In a classroom setting, a teacher might use Microsoft Forms to conduct quizzes. By exporting the responses to Excel, the teacher can quickly calculate the average score, identify the most frequently missed questions, and determine which students may need additional help.

- Additionally, the teacher can create a performance dashboard in Excel that tracks student progress over time.

2. Customer Satisfaction Surveys:

- A business might conduct customer satisfaction surveys using Microsoft Forms. After exporting the responses to Excel, the business can analyze the feedback to identify common trends, such as frequent complaints or highly praised services.

- The business can then create charts to visualize customer satisfaction trends over time and present these findings in meetings or reports.

3. Event Feedback Forms:

- After hosting an event, organizers might distribute a feedback form to attendees. By exporting the data to Excel, the organizers can filter responses to see feedback from different types of attendees (e.g., VIPs vs. general admission).

- They can also use PivotTables to cross-analyze feedback with demographic data, such as age or location, to tailor future events better.

Best Practices for Exporting Data

When exporting and using data in Excel, consider the following best practices to ensure data integrity and maximize the usefulness of your analysis:

1. Regularly Back Up Your Data:

- Always keep a backup copy of your original data before making any modifications. This ensures that you can revert to the original dataset if necessary.

2. Use Consistent Data Formats:

- Ensure that data formats are consistent throughout your Excel file. For example, dates should all follow the same format, and numerical data should be stored as numbers, not text.

3. Document Your Process:

- If you apply complex formulas, filters, or transformations to your data, document these steps. This will help you or others understand the process and replicate it if needed.

4. Ensure Data Privacy:

- When exporting and sharing data, be mindful of privacy concerns. Remove or anonymize sensitive information, especially when dealing with personal data or proprietary business information.

5. Leverage Excel's Collaboration Features:

- If you are working in a team, consider using Excel's collaboration features, such as co-authoring in real-time via OneDrive, to work together on data analysis and reporting.

Conclusion

Exporting data from Microsoft Forms to Excel is a crucial step for anyone looking to perform in-depth data analysis, create customized reports, or share insights with others. Excel's extensive array of tools and features enables you to transform raw survey or quiz data into actionable information. By following the steps and best practices outlined above, you can effectively manage your exported data, gaining deeper insights and making more informed decisions based on your Microsoft Forms responses.

4.3.2 Using Data in Other Applications

Microsoft Forms provides a versatile platform for collecting responses, whether you're gathering survey feedback, quiz results, or general information. However, the true power of data lies in how you can use it to derive insights, make decisions, and drive action. While exporting data to Excel is a crucial step, the possibilities for utilizing that data extend far beyond spreadsheet manipulation. Integrating your Microsoft Forms data with other applications can significantly enhance its value, enabling you to automate processes, perform advanced analytics, and share results with a broader audience.

In this section, we'll explore various ways you can leverage Microsoft Forms data in other applications, from popular Microsoft 365 tools to third-party services. These integrations can streamline your workflow, provide deeper insights, and facilitate better collaboration.

Integrating with Microsoft Power BI

One of the most powerful tools for data visualization and analysis within the Microsoft ecosystem is Power BI. By integrating your Microsoft Forms data with Power BI, you can create interactive dashboards that provide real-time insights into your collected responses.

a. Setting Up Data in Power BI:

To begin, you'll need to export your Forms data to Excel or directly to Power BI. If you choose the Excel route, save your spreadsheet in a OneDrive folder. Then, in Power BI, you can import this Excel file. Alternatively, if your organization uses Power Automate, you can set up an automatic flow that feeds your Form responses directly into Power BI.

b. Creating Dashboards and Reports:

Once your data is in Power BI, you can use its powerful visualization tools to create dashboards that highlight key metrics, such as response trends, demographic breakdowns, or satisfaction scores. The ability to filter and segment data dynamically allows you to drill down into specifics, providing a granular understanding of your results.

c. Automating Data Refresh:

Power BI offers options to automatically refresh your data at regular intervals, ensuring that your dashboards always display the most up-to-date information. This is particularly useful for ongoing surveys or forms where real-time monitoring is essential.

Leveraging Microsoft SharePoint for Collaboration

Microsoft SharePoint is another robust tool within the Microsoft 365 suite that can be used to share and collaborate on data collected via Microsoft Forms. By storing your Forms data in SharePoint, you create a central repository that can be accessed and edited by team members, ensuring everyone is working with the same information.

a. Storing Data in SharePoint Lists:

You can create a SharePoint list to capture data directly from Microsoft Forms. This is especially useful for organizations that use SharePoint as a document management system or intranet. By doing so, every new form submission automatically populates the SharePoint list, which can then be used to trigger workflows, generate reports, or be part of a larger project management system.

b. Collaborating and Sharing Insights:

Once your data is in SharePoint, you can leverage its collaboration features to share insights with your team. For example, you can set permissions to allow different team members to view, edit, or comment on the data. Additionally, SharePoint's integration with Microsoft Teams enables you to embed lists directly into Teams channels, making it easy to discuss and collaborate on responses in real-time.

c. Automating Processes with Power Automate:

Using Power Automate, you can create workflows that link Microsoft Forms with SharePoint. For instance, you can automate email notifications to team members when a new response is submitted, update records in a SharePoint list, or even generate tasks in Microsoft Planner based on specific responses. This level of automation can significantly enhance productivity by reducing the need for manual data entry and follow-ups.

Enhancing Communication with Microsoft Teams

Microsoft Teams is increasingly becoming the hub for teamwork in many organizations. By integrating Microsoft Forms with Teams, you can streamline communication and ensure that responses are acted upon quickly.

a. Embedding Forms in Teams:

You can embed Microsoft Forms directly into a Teams channel, allowing team members to fill out forms and surveys without leaving the Teams environment. This is particularly useful for gathering feedback during meetings or for quick polls within a team.

b. Monitoring Responses in Real-Time:

Teams also allows you to monitor responses in real-time by integrating Forms with your channels. For example, by setting up a Power Automate flow, you can receive notifications in a Teams channel each time a form is submitted. This immediate visibility ensures that critical responses are not missed and can be addressed promptly.

c. Facilitating Discussions Based on Responses:

After collecting responses, you can use Teams to discuss the results and decide on next steps. For instance, a survey on employee satisfaction can be reviewed by the HR team within Teams, allowing for collaborative analysis and brainstorming on how to address any issues raised.

Automating Workflows with Power Automate

Power Automate, formerly known as Microsoft Flow, is a powerful tool that allows you to automate workflows across various applications, including Microsoft Forms. By connecting Forms with other apps and services, you can streamline processes, reduce manual tasks, and ensure that your data is put to work efficiently.

a. Creating Automated Flows:

With Power Automate, you can set up flows that trigger actions based on form responses. For example, when a new response is submitted, Power Automate can send a customized email to the respondent, update a record in SharePoint, or even create a new task in Microsoft Planner. These automated workflows help save time and reduce the risk of human error.

b. Multi-Step Workflows:

Power Automate allows you to create complex workflows that involve multiple steps and conditions. For example, you can create a workflow that sends different email notifications based on the answers to specific form questions, or that routes responses to different departments for follow-up. This flexibility makes it possible to handle a wide range of scenarios, from simple acknowledgments to sophisticated data processing.

c. Integrating with Third-Party Apps:

Power Automate also supports integration with a wide array of third-party applications, such as Salesforce, Slack, or Dropbox. This means you can extend the capabilities of Microsoft Forms beyond the Microsoft ecosystem, allowing you to send form data to your CRM system, post responses in a Slack channel, or store attachments in a cloud storage service.

Using Microsoft Excel for Advanced Analysis

While we have already discussed exporting data to Excel, it is important to delve deeper into how you can use Excel for advanced data analysis and reporting. Excel's robust features make it a powerful tool for transforming raw form data into actionable insights.

a. Pivot Tables and Charts:

One of Excel's most powerful features is the Pivot Table, which allows you to summarize and analyze large datasets easily. You can use Pivot Tables to cross-tabulate responses, analyze trends, and identify patterns. Pivot Charts can then be used to visualize this data, making it easier to present your findings to stakeholders.

b. Advanced Formulas and Functions:

Excel offers a wide range of functions and formulas that can be used to manipulate and analyze your data. From simple functions like SUM and AVERAGE to more complex ones like VLOOKUP, INDEX/MATCH, or statistical functions, Excel enables you to perform detailed calculations that can uncover insights not immediately apparent in the raw data.

c. Data Cleaning and Transformation:

Before analysis, you may need to clean and transform your data. Excel's data tools, such as Text to Columns, Remove Duplicates, and Data Validation, can help you prepare your dataset for analysis by ensuring consistency and accuracy. You can also use Power Query to automate data cleaning and transformation processes, which is particularly useful if you regularly collect data using Microsoft Forms.

Connecting to External Databases

In some cases, your organization might use an external database to manage large volumes of data. Microsoft Forms data can be integrated with these databases, allowing for centralized data management and more sophisticated analysis.

a. Importing Data into SQL Server:

If your organization uses SQL Server, you can import your Microsoft Forms data into a SQL database. This can be done using a combination of Excel (as an intermediary) and SQL Server Management Studio (SSMS). Once your data is in SQL Server, you can leverage SQL queries to perform complex data analysis, create reports, or integrate with other applications.

b. Using Microsoft Access for Small-Scale Databases:

For smaller datasets, Microsoft Access provides a more accessible database solution. You can import your Forms data into Access, where you can create queries, forms, and reports. Access is particularly useful for managing datasets that require frequent updates or that need to be shared across multiple users.

c. Automating Data Sync with Power Automate:

If your organization requires regular data syncing between Microsoft Forms and an external database, Power Automate can be set up to automate this process. For example, you can create a flow that automatically updates your SQL Server database every time a new response is submitted in Microsoft Forms.

Third-Party Analytics and Business Intelligence Tools

Beyond the Microsoft ecosystem, there are numerous third-party tools that can be used to analyze and visualize Microsoft Forms data. These tools can offer specialized features and functionalities that might better suit your specific needs.

a. Tableau:

Tableau is a leading business intelligence tool known for its powerful data visualization capabilities. You can import your Microsoft Forms data into Tableau to create interactive dashboards and reports that offer deep insights into your responses. Tableau's advanced visualization options and ease of use make it an excellent choice for organizations that require detailed, customizable reports.

b. Google Data Studio:

Google Data Studio is a free tool that allows you to create dynamic reports and dashboards. While it's part of the Google ecosystem, you can still import your Microsoft Forms data (after exporting it to Excel or Google Sheets) to create visually appealing and interactive reports. Data Studio's real-time collaboration features are particularly useful for teams that need to work together on data analysis.

c. Zapier:

Zapier is an automation tool that connects different applications and services. With Zapier, you can create "Zaps" that automatically send your Microsoft Forms data to other tools like

Google Sheets, Salesforce, or Slack. This integration can help streamline your workflow, ensuring that your form responses are instantly available in the applications you use most.

Enhancing Data Security and Compliance

When using Microsoft Forms data in other applications, it's crucial to consider data security and compliance, especially if you are handling sensitive information. The following best practices can help ensure that your data remains secure throughout the process.

a. Data Encryption:

Ensure that all data transfers between Microsoft Forms and other applications are encrypted. This can typically be managed through your organization's IT policies, ensuring that data in transit is protected against unauthorized access.

b. Compliance with Regulations:

Depending on your industry, you may need to comply with regulations such as GDPR, HIPAA, or CCPA when handling form data. Make sure that any integration or third-party application you use adheres to these regulations, particularly regarding data storage, processing, and access.

c. Access Control:

Limit access to the data based on the principle of least privilege. Only those individuals who need access to the data should have it, and roles should be clearly defined to prevent unauthorized access. This is particularly important when integrating with third-party applications or when sharing data across departments.

This comprehensive section on using Microsoft Forms data in other applications highlights the versatility and power of Microsoft Forms when integrated with other tools. By taking advantage of these integrations, users can maximize the value of their data, automate processes, and ensure that their form responses are not only collected but actively utilized to drive decisions and actions within their organizations.

CHAPTER V
Creating Quizzes with Microsoft Forms

5.1 Setting Up a Quiz

5.1.1 Quiz vs. Survey

When embarking on the journey of creating forms in Microsoft Forms, one of the most important distinctions to understand is the difference between a quiz and a survey. Although both tools are essential for gathering information, they serve different purposes and offer distinct features tailored to their specific use cases.

Understanding the Purpose

Quizzes are designed primarily for assessment purposes. Whether in an educational setting, corporate training, or skill evaluation, quizzes are meant to measure knowledge, skills, or understanding of a particular subject. The core characteristic of a quiz is that it provides immediate feedback to the respondent based on predefined correct answers. This feedback can be as simple as indicating whether an answer was correct or incorrect, or as detailed as offering explanations for each answer. The scoring mechanism in quizzes allows for a clear, quantifiable measure of the respondent's performance, making quizzes an excellent tool for learning assessments, certifications, and even gamified experiences.

Surveys, on the other hand, are designed to collect opinions, feedback, or information without necessarily having right or wrong answers. They are more flexible in nature, accommodating a broader range of question types and response formats. The primary goal of a survey is to gather data for analysis, be it customer satisfaction, market research, employee engagement, or any other form of feedback. Unlike quizzes, surveys typically do not provide immediate feedback to respondents, as they are often used for data collection rather than assessment. The analysis of survey data is usually performed after responses have been gathered, often through statistical tools or qualitative analysis.

Structural Differences

The structure of a quiz differs significantly from that of a survey. In a quiz, questions are designed with specific correct answers in mind, and respondents are scored based on their answers. This scoring system can be used to determine pass/fail criteria, rank participants, or identify areas of strength and weakness. Each question in a quiz is usually followed by instant feedback, which can be customized to provide further learning opportunities or reinforce key concepts.

In contrast, surveys are generally more open-ended. While they can include multiple-choice questions, they also allow for a wide range of response types, including text boxes, rating scales, and more. Surveys may ask respondents to provide opinions, rate their satisfaction, or share experiences, with the focus being on the quality and depth of the data collected rather than scoring or assessment. Because surveys are often anonymous or confidential, they encourage honest and thoughtful responses, which are critical for generating accurate insights.

User Interaction and Experience

The user experience of quizzes and surveys also differs significantly. Quizzes are often more interactive, with elements such as timers, progress indicators, and instant feedback contributing to an engaging, game-like experience. This interactivity is crucial for keeping respondents motivated and focused, particularly in educational or training environments. The ability to provide instant feedback is not only beneficial for the respondent's learning but also for maintaining their interest and engagement throughout the quiz.

Surveys, while still interactive, tend to focus more on user convenience and ease of response. The design of surveys prioritizes accessibility and user-friendliness, ensuring that respondents can complete them quickly and without unnecessary complexity. Features such as skip logic and branching can be used to guide respondents through the survey in a way that is relevant to their experience or opinions, thereby enhancing the quality of the data collected.

Scoring and Feedback Mechanisms

In quizzes, scoring is an integral part of the process. Each question is assigned a specific point value, and the respondent's total score is calculated based on the number of correct answers. This score can then be used to evaluate the respondent's performance against a predefined standard or benchmark. In some cases, quizzes can be configured to provide different types of feedback based on the respondent's score, such as congratulatory messages for high scores or suggestions for improvement for lower scores.

Surveys, on the other hand, do not typically involve scoring. While some surveys may include questions that could be scored (e.g., knowledge checks within a broader survey), the primary focus is on gathering data rather than assessing performance. The feedback in surveys is usually more focused on expressing gratitude for participation or providing insights based on aggregate data once all responses have been collected and analyzed.

Application and Use Cases

The choice between using a quiz or a survey largely depends on the specific goals of the form you are creating. Quizzes are ideal for situations where you need to assess knowledge, certify skills, or provide educational feedback. For instance, teachers can use quizzes to evaluate student learning, trainers can use them to test participants' understanding of course material, and employers can use them to certify employee competencies.

Surveys, on the other hand, are better suited for gathering feedback, opinions, or data from a large audience. They are commonly used in customer satisfaction research, employee engagement studies, market research, and many other areas where understanding the experiences or opinions of a group is more important than assessing individual performance. Surveys allow for a broader range of data collection, making them a versatile tool for capturing insights that can inform decision-making, strategy, and improvement initiatives.

Conclusion: Choosing the Right Tool

Understanding the distinction between quizzes and surveys is crucial for effectively using Microsoft Forms to meet your objectives. Quizzes offer a structured, interactive, and feedback-driven experience, ideal for assessments and learning environments. Surveys provide a flexible, respondent-centered approach to data collection, suited for a wide range of research and feedback scenarios.

When deciding between creating a quiz or a survey in Microsoft Forms, consider the purpose of your form, the type of data you need to collect, and the experience you want to provide for your respondents. By choosing the right tool for the job, you can ensure that your form not only meets its objectives but also engages your audience in a meaningful and effective way.

5.1.2 Creating a New Quiz

Creating a new quiz in Microsoft Forms is a straightforward process that allows educators, trainers, and professionals to assess knowledge, gather feedback, and engage participants interactively. This section will guide you step-by-step through the process of setting up a new quiz, from the initial creation to configuring essential settings.

Step 1: Accessing Microsoft Forms

To start creating your quiz, you need to access Microsoft Forms:

1. Open Microsoft Forms: Go to forms.office.com or open Microsoft Forms from your Office 365 dashboard.

2. Sign in: Log in with your Microsoft account credentials. If you are part of an organization, use your work or school account.

3. Navigate to the Forms Interface: Once logged in, you will be directed to the Forms home page, where you can see your existing forms and quizzes.

Step 2: Starting a New Quiz

1. Create New Quiz: On the Microsoft Forms home page, click the "New Quiz" button. This will open a blank quiz template where you can begin building your quiz.

2. Name Your Quiz: The first step in creating your quiz is to give it a name. Click on the title placeholder, labeled "Untitled quiz", and enter a descriptive name for your quiz. This name should be clear and concise, reflecting the content or purpose of the quiz.

- Example: If the quiz is about basic mathematics, you might name it "Basic Math Skills Assessment."

3. Add a Description (Optional): Directly below the quiz title, you have the option to add a description. This is where you can provide instructions or additional information that quiz takers should know before starting the quiz.

- Example: "Please answer all questions to the best of your ability. This quiz is timed, and you will have 30 minutes to complete it."

Step 3: Adding Questions to Your Quiz

Now that your quiz framework is set up, the next step is to add questions. Microsoft Forms offers various question types that you can use to create an engaging and effective quiz.

1. Adding the First Question:

- Click on the "Add new" button to begin adding your first question. A drop-down menu will appear, giving you options to choose different types of questions such as Multiple Choice, Text, Rating, and Date.

- Since quizzes typically require more structured answers, the most commonly used question types are Multiple Choice, True or False, and Short Answer.

2. Choosing a Question Type:

- Select the appropriate question type for your first question. For example, choose Multiple Choice if you want the respondents to select one or more options from a list.

3. Entering the Question Text:

- After selecting the question type, a text box labeled "Question" will appear. Enter the question you want to ask your respondents.

- Example: "What is the capital of France?"

4. Providing Answer Options:

- Depending on the question type, you will need to provide answer options. For a multiple-choice question, click on "Option 1" and enter the first possible answer. Continue adding options by clicking "Add option".

- Example:

- Option 1: Paris

- Option 2: London

- Option 3: Rome

- Option 4: Berlin

5. Marking the Correct Answer:

   - Once you've entered all answer options, indicate the correct answer by clicking the checkmark next to the correct option.

   - Example: Click the checkmark next to "Paris" to indicate that it is the correct answer.

6. Adding Answer Feedback (Optional):

   - You can provide feedback for each answer choice. This is particularly useful in educational settings, as it allows learners to understand why an answer was correct or incorrect.

   - To add feedback, click on the "Message" icon next to each answer option and type in your feedback.

   - Example: "Paris is the capital of France, known for its art, culture, and history."

Step 4: Configuring Question Settings

Each question in your quiz can be customized further to meet your specific needs:

1. Requiring an Answer:

   - To ensure that respondents answer a particular question, toggle the "Required" option. This makes it mandatory for quiz takers to answer the question before moving on to the next one.

2. Allowing Multiple Answers:

   - If you're using a multiple-choice question and want to allow respondents to select more than one answer, toggle the "Multiple answers" option.

3. Shuffling Answer Options:

- For quizzes where you want to prevent respondents from simply memorizing the order of answers, you can enable the "Shuffle options" feature. This will randomize the order of the answer choices each time the quiz is taken.

Step 5: Adding More Questions

1. Adding Subsequent Questions:

- After creating your first question, click on the "Add new" button again to add more questions. Repeat the process outlined above for each new question.

2. Using Different Question Types:

- To create a more dynamic quiz, consider using a variety of question types. For instance, after a few multiple-choice questions, you might add a True or False question, or a Short Answer question where respondents must type in their answer.

  - *True or False Example:*

    - Question: "The Earth is flat."

    - Options: True, False

    - Correct Answer: False

  - *Short Answer Example:*

    - Question: "What is the sum of 8 and 5?"

    - Correct Answer: 13

    - Note: Short Answer questions allow you to specify a correct response, which the system will automatically check when grading.

3. Organizing Questions:

- You can rearrange questions by dragging them into the desired order. This allows you to organize your quiz logically, perhaps starting with easier questions and gradually increasing the difficulty.

Step 6: Customizing Quiz Settings

Before finalizing your quiz, there are several settings you should configure to ensure it meets your needs:

1. Setting Quiz Scoring:

   - Microsoft Forms automatically assigns points to quiz questions. You can adjust the point value for each question by clicking on the "Points" field next to the question and entering the desired number of points.

   - Consider the difficulty and importance of each question when assigning points.

   - Example: A difficult question might be worth 5 points, while an easier one is worth 1 point.

2. Enabling Automatic Grading:

   - For most question types, Microsoft Forms allows for automatic grading. When the quiz is completed, the system will automatically calculate the score based on the correct answers provided.

   - This feature is particularly useful for large groups of respondents, as it saves time on manual grading.

3. Adding a Custom Thank You Message:

   - After participants submit their quiz, you can display a custom thank you message. This can be used to acknowledge their effort and provide additional instructions or feedback.

   - To set this up, click on the "More form settings" (three dots in the upper right corner), select "Settings", and scroll down to "Thank you message".

4. Randomizing Question Order:

   - To further enhance the quiz's integrity, especially in a testing environment, you can shuffle the order of questions for each respondent. This prevents any potential cheating by ensuring that no two quizzes are identical.

5. Setting a Time Limit:

   - If your quiz is time-sensitive, you can use third-party tools or integrations to enforce a time limit. While Microsoft Forms doesn't have a built-in timer, you can manage time externally or through learning management systems that integrate with Microsoft Forms.

Step 7: Previewing Your Quiz

Before sharing your quiz with respondents, it's essential to preview it to ensure everything is set up correctly:

1. Preview Mode:

   - Click on the "Preview" button at the top of the form editor. This will allow you to see the quiz from the respondent's perspective on both desktop and mobile devices.

   - Go through the quiz as if you were a respondent, checking each question, answer option, and feedback message for accuracy.

2. Testing the Quiz:

   - Submit a test response to see how the quiz performs. Check that the scoring, feedback, and thank you message function as expected.

Step 8: Sharing Your Quiz

Once you're satisfied with your quiz, you're ready to share it with participants:

1. Generating a Shareable Link:

   - Click on "Share" at the top of the form editor. You will be given several options for distributing your quiz.

   - The default method is to share a link. Click "Copy" next to the generated link, and you can then paste this link into an email, a website, or a social media post.

2. Embedding the Quiz:

   - If you want to embed the quiz directly into a webpage or learning platform, select the "Embed" option. Copy the provided HTML code and paste it into your website's code where you want the quiz to appear.

3. Sharing via Email:

- Microsoft Forms allows you to send the quiz directly via email. Select the "Email" option, enter the email addresses of your participants, and add any message you want to include before sending.

4. Setting Response Options:

- Before finalizing the distribution, ensure your response settings align with your quiz's objectives. Decide whether respondents can submit multiple responses, if they need to be signed in, and whether their names should be collected automatically.

Step 9: Collecting and Reviewing Responses

After your quiz has been shared and responses start coming in, you can begin to review the data:

1. Viewing Responses:

- Click on the "Responses" tab in the quiz editor. Here, you can see a summary of responses, including how many people have completed the quiz, their scores, and the distribution of answers for each question.

2. Exporting Results:

- For more detailed analysis, export the responses to Excel by clicking "Open in Excel". This allows you to manipulate the data, generate charts, and further analyze the results.

3. Providing Additional Feedback:

- If needed, manually review responses and provide additional feedback, particularly for questions that require subjective answers or explanations.

Final Thoughts on Creating Quizzes

Creating a quiz in Microsoft Forms is an intuitive process that empowers educators, trainers, and professionals to assess and engage their audience effectively. By carefully crafting your questions, configuring settings, and previewing your quiz before sharing, you can ensure a smooth and successful experience for both you and your participants.

5.2 Adding Quiz Questions

Adding well-crafted questions is crucial for creating effective quizzes in Microsoft Forms. This section delves into the various types of questions you can include in your quiz, how to set them up, and best practices to ensure they are both engaging and effective. We'll explore each question type in detail, including practical tips for usage and considerations for creating a comprehensive quiz experience.

5.2.1 Question Types for Quizzes

Microsoft Forms offers a range of question types that can be utilized to build engaging and interactive quizzes. Understanding the nuances of each type allows you to select the most appropriate questions for your quiz objectives. Below, we will examine the most commonly used question types and their best practices.

Multiple Choice

Overview:

The Multiple Choice question type is one of the most versatile and commonly used question types in Microsoft Forms. It allows quiz creators to provide a list of options from which respondents can choose one or more answers. This type of question is useful for assessing knowledge, preferences, and opinions.

How to Create:

1. Add Question: Click on the "Add question" button and select "Multiple choice" from the list of question types.

2. Enter Question Text: Type the question you want to ask. Be clear and concise to avoid confusion.

3. Provide Options: Enter the possible answers in the provided fields. You can add as many options as needed.

4. Set Correct Answer: If you want to grade the quiz automatically, mark the correct answer(s) by selecting the appropriate option.

5. Allow Multiple Answers (if needed): If the question allows multiple answers, toggle the switch to enable this option.

Best Practices:

- Keep It Clear: Ensure that each option is distinct and does not overlap with others.

- Use Randomization: Randomize the order of answer options to prevent bias from the order in which options are presented.

- Limit the Number of Choices: Too many options can overwhelm respondents. Aim for 4-5 choices for optimal results.

Example:

Question: What are the primary colors in the RGB color model?

- Red

- Green

- Blue

- Yellow

True or False

Overview:

The True or False question type is straightforward and used for questions with binary answers. It is effective for testing basic understanding or factual knowledge.

How to Create:

1. Add Question: Click on "Add question" and choose "Yes/No" (which serves as True/False).

2. Enter Question Text: Clearly state the statement or question that requires a True or False response.

3. Mark Correct Answer: Indicate which response is correct (True or False).

Best Practices:

- Be Direct: Formulate statements that are unequivocally true or false to avoid ambiguity.

- Provide Context: Ensure the question provides enough context so that respondents understand what they are evaluating.

Example:

Statement: The capital of France is Paris.

- True

- False

Short Answer

Overview:

Short Answer questions are used when you want respondents to provide a brief, open-ended response. This question type is ideal for testing recall, opinion, or requiring a specific piece of information.

How to Create:

1. Add Question: Click on "Add question" and select "Text" for a short answer question.

2. Enter Question Text: Pose a question that requires a brief written response.

3. Set Response Validation (if needed): You can set up rules to limit the length of responses or validate responses based on specific criteria.

Best Practices:

- Be Specific: Clearly define what you expect in the response to avoid vague answers.

- Keep It Concise: Focus on questions that can be answered succinctly to keep the quiz manageable.

Example:

Question: What is the chemical symbol for water?

5.2.2 Adding Answer Feedback

Incorporating feedback into your quiz questions is a powerful tool to enhance the learning experience. Feedback provides immediate reinforcement, guiding respondents on their understanding of the material and helping them learn from their mistakes. Microsoft Forms offers flexible options for adding feedback, which can be customized to suit the needs of your quiz.

Understanding the Importance of Feedback

Before diving into the technical steps of adding feedback, it's important to understand why feedback matters. In educational and training settings, feedback serves several key purposes:

- Reinforcement of Learning: When respondents receive feedback, it reinforces the correct information and clarifies any misunderstandings. This is especially useful in formative assessments where the goal is to promote learning.

- Motivation: Positive feedback can boost a learner's confidence and motivation, encouraging them to continue with the quiz or other learning activities.

- Error Correction: Feedback on incorrect answers helps learners understand why their response was wrong, which can be crucial in mastering the subject matter.

- Customization: Feedback can be tailored to the specific needs of your audience, providing additional resources or explanations as needed.

Steps to Add Feedback in Microsoft Forms

Adding feedback to quiz questions in Microsoft Forms is straightforward and can be done for each type of question you include in your quiz. Below are the steps to add feedback for different question types:

Adding Feedback to Multiple Choice Questions

1. Create or Edit a Multiple Choice Question:

   - When you add a multiple-choice question, you'll have options to input the question and the possible answers.

2. Access Feedback Options:

   - After entering your question and answers, hover over each answer option. You will see a small comment icon (typically represented by a speech bubble or pencil icon). Clicking this icon allows you to add feedback specific to that answer.

3. Enter Feedback for Correct and Incorrect Answers:

   - For correct answers, you can add reinforcing feedback. For example, if the question is, "What is the capital of France?" and the correct answer is "Paris," the feedback could be, "Correct! Paris is the capital of France."

   - For incorrect answers, provide informative feedback that guides the learner. For example, if the answer "London" is chosen, the feedback might be, "Incorrect. London is the capital of the United Kingdom, not France."

4. Preview the Feedback:

   - Before finalizing your quiz, use the preview function to test how the feedback will appear to respondents. This ensures that your feedback is clear and appropriately placed.

5. Save and Continue:

   - Once satisfied, save the feedback and proceed to the next question or quiz setup step.

Adding Feedback to True or False Questions

1. Create a True or False Question:

   - Similar to multiple-choice questions, start by entering your True or False question.

2. Add Feedback to True and False Options:

   - Click on the feedback icon next to the "True" or "False" options.

   - For the correct answer, provide positive reinforcement. For example, if the statement is, "The Earth revolves around the Sun," and "True" is the correct answer, the feedback might be, "Correct! The Earth does revolve around the Sun, which is why we experience seasons."

   - For the incorrect answer, offer a brief explanation or corrective feedback. If "False" is selected, the feedback could be, "Incorrect. The Earth does indeed revolve around the Sun, which is a fundamental aspect of our solar system."

3. Test and Finalize:

   - As with multiple-choice questions, preview your quiz to ensure that the feedback is working as intended, then save your changes.

Adding Feedback to Short Answer Questions

1. Set Up a Short Answer Question:

   - Short answer questions require respondents to type in their answer. Start by crafting the question.

2. Add Automatic Feedback:

   - For short answer questions, feedback is typically provided based on the exact match of the typed answer. While Microsoft Forms allows for some variations, the feedback will be most effective if the correct answer is straightforward (e.g., "What is 2 + 2?").

   - You can add feedback for a range of accepted answers by entering possible correct answers in the form setup and associating feedback with each.

3. Provide General Feedback:

- If the answer does not match any of the expected responses, you can provide general feedback. This feedback could be something like, "The correct answer is 4. Remember to check your calculations."

4. Manual Review and Feedback:

- For more complex short answers, you might need to review responses manually and provide feedback after the quiz is completed. This can be done by exporting the responses and communicating feedback through another platform.

Adding Feedback to Ranking Questions

1. Set Up a Ranking Question:

- Ranking questions require respondents to order items based on criteria you set. Begin by defining the items and their correct order.

2. Access Feedback Options:

- For ranking questions, feedback can be provided on whether the order was correct or incorrect.

3. Offer Detailed Feedback:

- If the respondent ranks the items correctly, you can offer feedback that reinforces the correct reasoning behind the order. For example, "Well done! Ranking the planets by size correctly helps in understanding their physical properties."

- If the ranking is incorrect, provide constructive feedback that explains the correct order and why it's important. For example, "Incorrect. Mercury is smaller than Earth, so it should be ranked lower."

4. Save and Preview:

- Always preview how the feedback will appear and test different ranking scenarios to ensure your feedback is accurate and informative.

Providing Feedback on Open Text Questions

1. Create an Open Text Question:

- Open text questions allow respondents to answer in their own words. These questions are more subjective and often require manual review.

2. General Feedback:

- Since Microsoft Forms does not automatically grade open text responses, you can set up general feedback that applies to all answers, such as, "Thank you for your response! Please review the study materials if you need more clarity."

3. Post-Quiz Feedback:

- After the quiz, you may review the responses and provide individualized feedback. This can be done through email or another learning management system (LMS) where feedback can be more personalized.

Using Adaptive Feedback for Branching

1. Introduction to Branching Feedback:

- Branching allows you to customize the flow of the quiz based on the respondent's answers. This can be used to provide adaptive feedback, guiding the learner to more relevant content based on their previous responses.

2. Setting Up Branching:

- In the quiz settings, enable branching to direct respondents to different questions based on their answers. For example, if a respondent answers a question incorrectly, you might branch them to a question that revisits a related topic for reinforcement.

3. Crafting Branching Feedback:

- Branching feedback can be a powerful tool for remediation. For example, if a respondent answers a question about historical dates incorrectly, they might be branched to a series of questions that provide more context and background information.

4. Testing and Refining Branching Feedback:

- Preview the quiz to ensure the branching works smoothly and that the feedback provided at each step is clear and effective. Make adjustments as needed to optimize the learning experience.

Best Practices for Effective Feedback

Adding feedback is not just about correcting mistakes; it's an opportunity to deepen understanding and encourage ongoing learning. Here are some best practices for crafting effective feedback in your quizzes:

- Be Specific: Tailor your feedback to the question and the respondent's answer. Specific feedback is more likely to be remembered and applied.

- Keep it Constructive: Even when addressing incorrect answers, maintain a positive tone that encourages further learning rather than discouraging the respondent.

- Use Simple Language: Ensure that the language used in the feedback is clear and easy to understand, avoiding technical jargon unless it's essential and previously explained.

- Provide Additional Resources: Where possible, include links to additional resources or suggest further reading to reinforce learning.

- Balance Praise and Correction: While it's important to correct mistakes, also highlight what the respondent did well to maintain motivation.

Conclusion

Adding feedback to quiz questions in Microsoft Forms is a key step in creating an interactive and educational experience. By thoughtfully crafting feedback for each type of question, you can help guide learners through the material, reinforcing correct answers and providing valuable insights when mistakes are made. Whether you're creating a simple quiz or a comprehensive assessment, the feedback you provide can make all the difference in how your respondents engage with and learn from the content.

5.3 Scoring and Feedback

Scoring and feedback are critical elements of creating effective quizzes using Microsoft Forms. They help you evaluate the understanding and performance of respondents, and provide valuable insights for both educators and learners. In this section, we'll delve into the specifics of setting points for questions and providing automatic feedback.

5.3.1 Setting Points for Questions

Setting points for questions in Microsoft Forms is an essential step in creating a quiz that accurately reflects the importance and difficulty of each question. By assigning points, you can weight questions according to their significance and provide a clear grading structure for your quiz. This section will guide you through the process of setting points for questions in a Microsoft Forms quiz.

Understanding the Importance of Points

Points serve several purposes in a quiz:

- Differentiation: Points allow you to differentiate between questions based on their difficulty or importance.

- Motivation: Points can motivate respondents to put in their best effort, especially if the quiz results contribute to their overall evaluation.

- Clear Assessment: Points provide a clear framework for assessing performance, making it easier to interpret results.

Step-by-Step Guide to Setting Points

1. Access Your Quiz:

  - Open Microsoft Forms.

  - Navigate to the quiz you want to edit by selecting it from your list of forms.

2. Enter Edit Mode:

  - Click on the "Edit" button to enter the quiz's editing interface.

3. Select a Question:

  - Click on the question for which you want to set points. This will open the question's editing options.

4. Assign Points:

  - Locate the "Points" field, usually found at the top right of the question box.

  - Enter the number of points you want to assign to the question. This can be any positive number that reflects the question's weight in the quiz.

  - Repeat this process for each question in your quiz.

Tips for Effective Point Allocation

- Balance Difficulty and Importance:

  - Assign higher points to more difficult or important questions to reflect their significance in the overall assessment.

- Consistency:

  - Ensure that similar types of questions have consistent point values unless there is a specific reason to differentiate.

- Partial Credit:

  - Consider assigning partial points for multi-part questions or for partially correct answers if the question type allows for it.

Examples of Point Allocation

- Multiple Choice Questions:

  - Simple knowledge-based questions: 1 point each.

  - More complex analysis-based questions: 2-3 points each.

- True or False Questions:

 - Typically: 1 point each, unless they cover critical concepts, in which case they might be worth more.

- Short Answer Questions:

 - Basic definitions: 1-2 points each.

 - Detailed explanations or complex answers: 3-5 points each.

Reviewing Point Allocation

Once you have assigned points to all your questions, it's important to review the total points for the quiz. Ensure that the total points reflect the quiz's intended difficulty and that there is a reasonable balance between different types of questions. You can do this by:

- Summarizing Total Points:

 - Look at the total points for the quiz, usually displayed at the top of the quiz editing interface.

- Adjusting as Necessary:

 - If the total points seem too high or too low, adjust the points for individual questions accordingly.

Testing Your Quiz

Before finalizing your quiz, consider testing it to ensure that the point distribution is fair and effective. You can do this by:

- Previewing the Quiz:

 - Use the "Preview" feature to take the quiz yourself or ask a colleague to do so.

- Analyzing Results:

 - Look at the results to see if the points accurately reflect the difficulty and importance of each question.

Finalizing Points

Once you are satisfied with the point allocation, save your quiz. The points you have set will now be used to automatically calculate scores when respondents complete the quiz.

By carefully setting points for each question, you can create a balanced and effective quiz that accurately assesses the knowledge and skills of your respondents. Points provide a clear framework for both educators and learners, making the evaluation process transparent and meaningful.

5.3.2 Providing Automatic Feedback

Providing automatic feedback in Microsoft Forms is a powerful feature that enhances the quiz-taking experience by allowing users to receive immediate and customized responses based on their answers. This feature not only helps learners understand their mistakes but also reinforces correct answers, making quizzes more educational and interactive. In this section, we'll explore how to set up automatic feedback, best practices for creating effective feedback, and how to leverage this feature to improve the overall learning experience.

Understanding the Importance of Feedback

Before diving into the technical aspects of setting up automatic feedback, it's essential to understand why feedback is crucial in the context of quizzes. Feedback serves several purposes:

- Reinforcement of Learning: Immediate feedback reinforces what the respondent has learned, solidifying the correct answers in their memory.

- Error Correction: When a respondent answers a question incorrectly, feedback helps them understand why their answer was wrong and guides them toward the correct information.

- Motivation: Feedback, especially when positive, can motivate respondents to engage more deeply with the material and feel more confident in their knowledge.

- Personalized Learning: Feedback can be tailored to individual responses, making the learning experience more personalized and effective.

Given these benefits, it's clear that feedback should not be an afterthought but an integral part of quiz design.

Setting Up Automatic Feedback in Microsoft Forms

Microsoft Forms allows you to provide automatic feedback for each quiz question. This feedback can be customized based on whether the respondent answers correctly or incorrectly. Here's how to set it up:

1. Creating a Quiz Question:

   - Start by creating a quiz or editing an existing quiz in Microsoft Forms.

   - Add a new question by selecting the question type (e.g., Multiple Choice, True or False, Short Answer).

   - Enter the question text and possible answers.

2. Enabling Feedback:

   - Once you've entered the question and answer choices, you'll notice a section labeled "Add feedback" below each answer choice.

   - Click on "Add feedback" for each possible response.

3. Customizing Feedback:

   - For correct answers, provide positive reinforcement. This could be a simple "Correct!" or more detailed feedback explaining why the answer is correct.

   - For incorrect answers, guide the respondent towards the correct answer by explaining why their choice was wrong. You can also provide additional resources or hints to help them understand the concept better.

   - If the question is a Short Answer or similar type where the answer isn't pre-defined, you can provide general feedback based on the correct answer you expect.

4. Using Rich Text and Media in Feedback:

   - Microsoft Forms allows you to use rich text in feedback, so you can add emphasis through bold, italics, or underlining.

- Additionally, you can insert hyperlinks to direct respondents to further reading or videos, and even embed images or videos directly into the feedback.

5. Saving and Testing the Feedback:

  - After you've set up the feedback, save the question.

  - It's always a good idea to test your quiz to ensure that the feedback displays correctly and is helpful to respondents.

Best Practices for Providing Effective Feedback

To maximize the impact of your feedback, consider the following best practices:

1. Be Specific and Clear:

  - Specific feedback helps learners understand exactly what they got right or wrong. Avoid vague statements and focus on the key concept or mistake.

2. Keep Feedback Constructive:

  - Constructive feedback, especially for incorrect answers, is essential. Encourage learning by pointing out what could be improved or rethought, rather than just stating that the answer is wrong.

3. Use a Positive Tone:

  - Even when correcting mistakes, maintain a positive and encouraging tone. This helps keep learners motivated and engaged.

4. Align Feedback with Learning Objectives:

  - Ensure that your feedback is directly related to the learning objectives of the quiz. Reinforce the key concepts that you want the learner to remember.

5. Provide Additional Resources:

  - If appropriate, provide links to additional reading materials, videos, or other resources that can help the learner understand the topic more deeply.

6. Consider Different Learning Styles:

  - People learn in different ways. By incorporating different types of media into your feedback (e.g., text, images, videos), you can cater to a wider range of learning preferences.

Examples of Effective Feedback

To illustrate how to craft effective feedback, let's consider a few examples based on different types of quiz questions.

1. Multiple Choice Question:

   - Question: "Which of the following is the capital of France?"

   - Correct Answer: Paris

   - Correct Feedback: "Correct! Paris is the capital of France, known for its rich history, art, and culture."

   - Incorrect Feedback: "Incorrect. The correct answer is Paris. It's important to remember that Paris is not only the capital but also the largest city in France. Consider reviewing the capitals of major European countries for better understanding."

2. True or False Question:

   - Question: "The sun revolves around the Earth."

   - Correct Answer: False

   - Correct Feedback: "Well done! The Earth revolves around the sun, which is the center of our solar system."

   - Incorrect Feedback: "Incorrect. Actually, the Earth revolves around the sun. This is a fundamental concept in astronomy known as the heliocentric model."

3. Short Answer Question:

   - Question: "Name the process by which plants make their food."

   - Correct Answer: Photosynthesis

   - Correct Feedback: "Correct! Photosynthesis is the process by which plants use sunlight to convert carbon dioxide and water into glucose and oxygen."

   - Incorrect Feedback: "The correct answer is photosynthesis. This process is crucial for life on Earth as it is the foundation of the food chain. Review your notes on plant biology for more details."

Leveraging Feedback for Enhanced Learning Outcomes

Feedback isn't just about correcting mistakes; it's about guiding learners towards a deeper understanding of the material. When used effectively, feedback can transform a simple quiz into a powerful learning tool. Here are some strategies for leveraging feedback to enhance learning outcomes:

1. Use Feedback to Identify Knowledge Gaps:

- Analyze the feedback provided to see which areas learners struggle with the most. This can help you identify knowledge gaps and areas where further instruction is needed.

2. Encourage Reflection Through Feedback:

- Prompt learners to reflect on their answers and the feedback they receive. This can be done by asking follow-up questions or encouraging them to reattempt the quiz after reviewing the feedback.

3. Iterative Learning with Feedback:

- Design your quizzes to allow multiple attempts, with feedback helping learners improve each time. This iterative approach can lead to better retention and understanding of the material.

4. Gamify the Quiz Experience:

- Use feedback to gamify the quiz experience by awarding points or badges for correct answers or improvements. This can increase engagement and make learning more enjoyable.

5. Personalize Feedback Where Possible:

- If your audience is diverse, consider tailoring feedback to different learning levels or backgrounds. This can make the learning experience more relevant and impactful for each individual.

Measuring the Effectiveness of Feedback

To ensure that your feedback is achieving its intended goals, it's important to measure its effectiveness. Here are some ways to do this:

1. Monitor Quiz Performance Over Time:

- Track how learners' quiz scores improve over time after implementing feedback. This can provide insight into whether the feedback is helping learners grasp the material better.

2. Collect Learner Feedback:

- Ask learners directly about their experience with the quiz and the feedback they received. This can be done through follow-up surveys or informal discussions.

3. Analyze Response Patterns:

- Look at how often learners change their answers after receiving feedback. If learners consistently correct their mistakes, it suggests that the feedback is effective.

4. Adjust Feedback Based on Results:

- Use the data collected to refine and improve your feedback. If certain feedback isn't resonating with learners, consider rephrasing it or providing additional clarification.

Conclusion

Providing automatic feedback in Microsoft Forms quizzes is a feature that, when used thoughtfully, can significantly enhance the learning experience. By offering immediate, personalized, and constructive feedback, educators and quiz creators can guide learners through their mistakes, reinforce correct knowledge, and ultimately create a more engaging and effective learning environment.

Remember that feedback is not just about correcting errors—it's about nurturing growth, understanding, and confidence in your learners. By following the strategies and best practices outlined in this section, you can maximize the impact of your quizzes and help your audience achieve their learning goals.

CHAPTER VI
Advanced Features and Integrations

6.1 Using Forms with Microsoft Teams

6.1.1 Creating Forms in Teams

Microsoft Teams has become a central hub for collaboration in many organizations, and integrating Microsoft Forms into Teams enhances the way teams can collect and analyze data, conduct surveys, and engage in quizzes—all within the same platform. Creating forms directly in Teams is a powerful feature that streamlines the process, allowing users to stay within the context of their work without switching between applications.

In this section, we will walk through the process of creating forms in Microsoft Teams, highlighting the steps to ensure that your forms are set up efficiently and effectively.

1. Accessing Microsoft Forms in Teams

Before creating a form in Microsoft Teams, it is essential to understand where and how you can access Microsoft Forms within the Teams environment. Microsoft Forms can be integrated into Teams in several ways:

- Forms Tab in a Channel: You can add Forms as a tab in any channel within a team. This allows all team members to access, fill out, and analyze the form directly from the channel.

- Forms App: The Forms app can be added directly to Teams, providing easy access to create, view, and manage forms across different teams and channels.

- Forms Bot: The Forms bot can be used in chat to create quick polls and quizzes directly from within the chat window.

To get started with creating a form in Teams, follow these steps:

1. Open Microsoft Teams: Start by opening the Microsoft Teams application on your desktop or in a web browser. Ensure you are signed in with the correct credentials.

2. Navigate to Your Team: Choose the team and channel where you want to create the form. This is important because the form will be associated with this particular team and channel.

3. Add a New Tab: At the top of the channel, you'll see a "+" button. Click on it to add a new tab.

4. Select Forms: In the list of available apps, search for "Forms" and select it. This will allow you to add a Microsoft Forms tab to your channel.

5. Create a New Form or Quiz: You'll be given the option to either create a new form or quiz or choose an existing one to link to this tab.

2. Creating a New Form

Once you have added the Forms tab to your channel, you can proceed to create a new form. Here's how:

1. Choose to Create a New Form: After selecting Forms, click on "Create a new form." You will be taken to the form creation interface.

2. Title and Description: Start by giving your form a title. This should be concise yet descriptive enough to give users an idea of the form's purpose. You can also add a description to provide further details or instructions for those filling out the form.

3. Add Questions: Now, begin adding questions to your form. Microsoft Forms offers several question types, including:

  - Multiple Choice: Ideal for questions with predefined options. You can allow single or multiple selections.

  - Text: Use this for open-ended questions where users can type in their responses.

  - Rating: This allows respondents to rate something on a scale, which is great for gathering feedback.

- Date: Use this to collect date-related responses.

Each question type has its own set of options that you can configure, such as making a question required or adding a subtitle for more context.

4. Customizing Questions:

- Add Options: For multiple-choice questions, you can add as many options as needed. You can also enable the "Other" option to allow respondents to add their own answers.

- Branching Logic: If you want the form to adapt based on user responses, you can use branching. For example, if a respondent answers "Yes" to a question, you can direct them to a specific follow-up question.

5. Preview the Form: Before finalizing your form, it's important to preview it to ensure everything looks as expected. Click on "Preview" to see how the form will appear on both desktop and mobile devices.

3 Creating a Quiz

In addition to forms, you can also create quizzes in Microsoft Teams using Microsoft Forms. The process is similar, but with added functionality for scoring and feedback.

1. Select Quiz Option: When you click on the Forms tab, choose "Create a new quiz" instead of a form.

2. Set Up Quiz Questions: As with forms, you can add various types of questions. However, in quizzes, you have the option to assign points to each question and provide feedback for correct or incorrect answers.

3. Scoring and Feedback:

- Automatic Scoring: For multiple-choice and other closed-ended questions, you can set the correct answer(s) so that Forms can automatically score the quiz as responses come in.

- Provide Feedback: After a user submits their quiz, you can provide instant feedback. This could include explanations for why an answer was correct or incorrect, which is particularly useful in educational settings.

4. Customize Quiz Settings: You can also adjust the settings for your quiz, such as allowing respondents to see their results immediately after submission or showing correct answers.

4. Saving and Sharing Your Form

Once your form or quiz is complete, the next step is to save it and make it available to your team members.

1. Save the Form: Ensure you save your form by clicking "Save" at the top of the screen. This will ensure all your changes are kept.

2. Share with Team Members:

   - Post in the Channel: When you save your form, you have the option to post about it in the channel. This will notify team members that the form is available to fill out.

   - Share via Link: If you want to share the form outside of Teams or with a broader audience, you can generate a link to the form by clicking on "Share" and selecting "Copy link."

   - Adjust Permissions: By default, forms created in Teams are accessible only to team members, but you can adjust the sharing settings to allow anyone with the link to respond, if necessary.

5. Managing Forms in Teams

After your form or quiz has been shared, it's important to know how to manage it effectively.

1. Viewing Responses: You can view responses directly from the Forms tab in Teams. The interface provides a summary of responses as well as the ability to view individual submissions.

2. Exporting Data: If you need to analyze the data further, you can export responses to Excel. This option is available in the "Responses" tab.

3. Editing the Form: If you need to make changes to the form after it has been published, you can do so directly from the Forms tab. Be aware that changes will be reflected immediately to all users.

4. Closing the Form: Once you have collected the necessary responses, you may want to close the form to prevent further submissions. This can be done by changing the settings in the "Responses" tab.

6. Best Practices for Creating Forms in Teams

To maximize the effectiveness of your forms and quizzes in Microsoft Teams, consider the following best practices:

1. Keep Forms Simple: While it can be tempting to add many questions and options, keeping your form simple and focused will likely yield better response rates.

2. Test the Form: Before sharing the form widely, test it with a small group to ensure it functions as intended and is easy to understand.

3. Use Branching Judiciously: Branching can greatly enhance the user experience by keeping the form relevant to each respondent, but overcomplicating it can confuse users.

4. Monitor Responses Regularly: Keep an eye on the responses as they come in, especially if the form is being used for time-sensitive information gathering.

5. Communicate Clearly: Ensure that the purpose of the form and any instructions are clearly communicated to your team members to avoid confusion.

Conclusion

Creating forms within Microsoft Teams using Microsoft Forms is a powerful way to engage with your team, gather important information, and facilitate quizzes and surveys. By following the steps outlined in this section, you can create effective, user-friendly forms that will enhance collaboration and productivity in your team. Whether you're gathering feedback, conducting surveys, or assessing knowledge with quizzes, integrating Forms into Teams provides a seamless experience for both creators and respondents.

6.1.2 Managing Responses in Teams

Managing responses in Microsoft Teams when using Microsoft Forms is a critical part of the workflow, particularly for those who rely on collaboration and quick access to data. Integrating Microsoft Forms with Microsoft Teams provides a seamless experience for gathering, viewing, and analyzing responses in real time without needing to leave the Teams environment. In this section, we will delve into the step-by-step process of managing responses within Microsoft Teams, exploring various features that enhance productivity and collaboration.

Overview of Response Management in Microsoft Teams

Once a Microsoft Form has been created and distributed within a Teams channel, the next important step is to manage the incoming responses. The integration between Microsoft Forms and Teams allows for responses to be automatically compiled and accessible directly within Teams. This not only saves time but also facilitates easier collaboration among team members as they can review and discuss the results in one place.

Response management includes viewing responses, filtering and sorting data, analyzing results, and sharing insights with your team. Teams provides several tools and features that make these tasks straightforward and efficient.

Accessing Responses in Microsoft Teams

After creating and sharing your form, you can easily access the responses within Microsoft Teams. To do this:

1. Open the Relevant Team and Channel: Navigate to the Teams app and select the team and channel where the form was created or shared.

2. Locate the Form: You can find the form either in the conversation tab where it was originally posted or in the "Files" or "Tabs" section if it was added as a dedicated tab.

3. View Responses:

   - If the form is accessible through a tab, simply click on the tab, and you will see an option to view responses.

   - If you're accessing it from the conversation, click on the link provided in the conversation thread, which will direct you to the responses.

Responses are displayed in a summary format, providing an at-a-glance overview of the data. This summary typically includes charts, graphs, and tables that represent the collected data visually, making it easier to understand trends and patterns.

Detailed Analysis of Responses

While the summary view provides a quick snapshot of the data, detailed analysis may require a deeper dive into the responses. Microsoft Teams, integrated with Forms, allows you to drill down into the data:

1. View Individual Responses:

 - You can click on each response to see how individual respondents answered each question. This is particularly useful for qualitative data or when you need to track responses from specific individuals.

2. Use Filters:

 - Teams allows you to filter responses based on specific criteria. For example, you can filter by time range (responses from the last week), by respondent (see how a particular team or department responded), or by specific answers (view all respondents who chose a particular option).

3. Exporting Responses:

 - If you need to perform more advanced analysis, such as creating pivot tables or using formulas, you can export the data to Excel directly from Teams. Simply click on the "Open in Excel" option within the responses tab. This will download the data, preserving the formatting and allowing you to manipulate it as needed.

 - The exported Excel file will include all responses in a tabular format, with each respondent's answers listed in a separate row. This format is ideal for deeper analysis, especially when working with large datasets.

Collaboration on Responses

One of the key benefits of managing responses in Microsoft Teams is the ability to collaborate with your team in real time. Here's how Teams facilitates collaboration:

1. Discuss Responses in the Conversation Tab:

 - Once responses start coming in, team members can discuss the results directly in the Teams channel. This is particularly useful for brainstorming sessions, strategy meetings, or when immediate action is required based on the data.

- You can @mention specific team members to draw their attention to particular responses or insights.

2. Commenting on Responses:

   - If your form is set up as a tab, users can leave comments directly within the tab interface. These comments can be used to note observations, suggest actions, or raise questions about specific data points.

   - Comments can also be used for asynchronous collaboration, where team members can leave their thoughts for others to review later.

3. Real-Time Notifications:

   - Microsoft Teams can be configured to send notifications to the channel whenever a new response is received. This ensures that the team is always up to date with the latest data and can react promptly.

   - Notifications can be customized to include summaries of the responses or to trigger only for specific types of responses (e.g., when a critical issue is flagged by a respondent).

Automating Response Management with Power Automate

For teams that handle a large volume of responses or require a more automated approach to response management, integrating Microsoft Forms and Teams with Power Automate (formerly Microsoft Flow) can be highly beneficial. Power Automate allows you to create automated workflows that can streamline various aspects of response management. Here's how you can leverage Power Automate:

1. Automatic Alerts and Notifications:

   - Set up automated notifications for specific conditions. For example, you can create a workflow that sends an alert to a Teams channel or an individual team member whenever a response meets certain criteria (e.g., low satisfaction scores).

2. Automated Data Processing:

   - Power Automate can be used to automatically process the data as it comes in. For example, you can set up a workflow to automatically categorize responses based on certain keywords or to summarize data and post the summary to a Teams channel at the end of each day.

3. Archiving Responses:

- If your team deals with surveys that gather ongoing feedback, you might need to regularly archive older responses to keep the current dataset manageable. Power Automate can help by automatically exporting responses to a SharePoint list or a database and then clearing out the older data from Teams.

Ensuring Data Privacy and Security

Managing responses within Microsoft Teams also involves ensuring that the data is handled securely and in compliance with relevant privacy regulations. Here are some best practices to ensure data security:

1. Control Access to Responses:

- Make sure that only authorized team members have access to the form and its responses. You can control access by setting permissions in Teams and within Microsoft Forms itself.

- Consider using private channels in Teams if the data is sensitive and should only be visible to a subset of team members.

2. Data Encryption:

- Microsoft Forms and Teams use encryption to protect data both at rest and in transit. Ensure that these settings are enabled and compliant with your organization's security policies.

3. Regular Audits:

- Conduct regular audits of who has access to the responses and review any changes to permissions or data handling practices. This helps to ensure that no unauthorized access occurs and that your data management practices remain secure.

4. GDPR Compliance:

- If you are collecting data from individuals within the European Union, ensure that your data collection and management processes are GDPR-compliant. This includes informing respondents of how their data will be used, ensuring that data can be deleted upon request, and handling any data breaches in accordance with GDPR guidelines.

Sharing and Presenting Insights

Once you've analyzed the responses, the next step is often to share your insights with the team or stakeholders. Microsoft Teams offers several ways to do this effectively:

1. Presenting Data in Teams Meetings:

   - You can easily present the response data during a Teams meeting. Use the "Share" feature to display the response summary or the Excel analysis. This is particularly useful for discussing results during team meetings or stakeholder briefings.

2. Creating Reports:

   - If you've exported the data to Excel or another analysis tool, you can create detailed reports and then share them within the Teams channel. Upload the report file to the channel's "Files" tab or share it directly in the conversation.

3. Using Power BI for Visualizations:

   - For more advanced data visualization, you can import the response data into Power BI and create interactive dashboards. These dashboards can then be shared within Teams, allowing team members to explore the data dynamically.

   - Power BI also allows for embedding live dashboards into Teams channels, providing real-time insights as responses are collected.

Conclusion

Managing responses in Microsoft Teams when using Microsoft Forms is a powerful way to streamline data collection and analysis while enhancing team collaboration. The ability to access, analyze, and share response data within the same platform that your team uses for communication and collaboration ensures a more efficient workflow and better decision-making.

By leveraging the integration between Microsoft Forms and Teams, along with tools like Power Automate and Power BI, you can automate response management, ensure data security, and present insights in a compelling manner. Whether you're conducting simple surveys or complex data collection efforts, managing responses in Teams makes the process intuitive and effective.

6.2 Integrating with Other Microsoft 365 Apps

6.2.1 Forms and Excel

Microsoft Forms and Excel work seamlessly together, offering powerful tools for data collection and analysis. Integrating these two applications allows users to efficiently gather, organize, and analyze data, making it easier to make informed decisions. This section provides a comprehensive guide on how to use Microsoft Forms with Excel, from setting up data collection forms to analyzing responses in Excel.

1. Overview of Integration

Microsoft Forms and Excel integration is a robust feature that allows users to automatically export responses from a form into an Excel spreadsheet. This functionality is particularly useful for anyone who needs to collect data and analyze it using Excel's powerful data analysis tools.

When you create a form in Microsoft Forms, the responses can be directly linked to an Excel workbook. This integration ensures that every response is recorded in real-time, with data automatically structured in a way that's easy to work with in Excel. This real-time integration is beneficial for projects requiring ongoing data collection and analysis, such as surveys, quizzes, feedback forms, and more.

2. Creating a Form Linked to Excel

To start, it's important to know how to create a form in Microsoft Forms that is linked to an Excel spreadsheet:

1. Starting from Excel:

  - Open Excel and navigate to the "Insert" tab.

  - Select "Forms," then choose "New Form."

- This action will create a new form in Microsoft Forms that is automatically linked to the Excel workbook you started from. Every response submitted through this form will be recorded in this Excel workbook.

2. Starting from Microsoft Forms:

- Go to Microsoft Forms and create your form as usual by selecting "New Form" or "New Quiz."

- Once the form is created, you can export responses to Excel at any time by clicking the "Open in Excel" button on the responses tab. This will create an Excel file with all the current responses, and any new responses can be manually refreshed in Excel.

3. Working with Data in Excel

Once your form is connected to Excel, the real power of this integration comes into play with data analysis:

1. Data Structure in Excel:

- Each form response is recorded as a new row in the Excel spreadsheet.

- The first row contains the column headers, which correspond to the questions in your form.

- Each subsequent row represents a respondent's answers, with columns representing each question.

2. Automated Data Updates:

- If you started the form from Excel, the data updates automatically. Each new response submitted through the form appears in the Excel sheet as soon as it is received.

- If the form was created in Microsoft Forms, you would need to click "Open in Excel" from the Microsoft Forms portal to generate a new Excel file or update an existing one with new responses.

3. Using Excel Functions for Analysis:

- Sorting and Filtering: Excel allows you to sort and filter data by any column, making it easy to focus on specific responses or trends. For example, you can filter responses to see all those that answered a particular question in a specific way.

- Formulas and Calculations: Use Excel formulas to calculate averages, totals, or other statistics based on the form responses. For instance, if your form includes a quiz, you could calculate the average score across all respondents.

- Pivot Tables: Excel's Pivot Table feature is particularly useful for summarizing and analyzing data. You can create Pivot Tables to group responses, calculate totals, averages, or other statistics, and display data in a user-friendly format.

- Conditional Formatting: Use conditional formatting to highlight specific responses, such as all responses with a score below a certain threshold.

4. Advanced Excel Techniques

The integration with Excel also allows for more advanced data manipulation techniques:

1. Using Power Query for Data Cleaning:

- Power Query is an Excel tool that helps you clean and transform data. For example, if your form responses include text that needs to be standardized (e.g., converting all text to uppercase), you can use Power Query to automate this process.

2. Data Validation and Quality Control:

- Ensure the accuracy of your data by applying data validation rules in Excel. For instance, you can set up rules to flag any responses that fall outside of expected ranges or to identify duplicate responses.

3. Creating Dashboards and Reports:

- Excel is a powerful tool for creating interactive dashboards and reports. You can use charts, graphs, and slicers to visualize the data collected from your forms. For example, create a pie chart to show the distribution of responses to a particular question, or use a line graph to track changes in responses over time.

4. Using Excel's Analysis ToolPak:

 - The Analysis ToolPak is an Excel add-in that provides data analysis tools for statistical analysis. This is particularly useful for more complex data analysis tasks, such as running regressions, calculating moving averages, or conducting hypothesis testing on your form data.

5. Automating Tasks with Excel and Microsoft Forms

Excel's integration with Microsoft Forms also supports automation, enabling you to streamline repetitive tasks:

1. Automating Data Collection:

 - Use Excel's built-in scripting tools like VBA (Visual Basic for Applications) or newer Office Scripts (available in Excel Online) to automate the collection and analysis of form data. For example, you could create a script that automatically refreshes the data in your workbook every time a new response is received.

2. Using Power Automate for Workflow Automation:

 - Power Automate (formerly Microsoft Flow) can be used to create workflows that automate tasks between Microsoft Forms and Excel. For example, you can set up a flow that sends an email notification every time a form response meets certain criteria (e.g., a low quiz score), or automatically copies data from your Excel sheet to another location for further processing.

3. Triggering Actions Based on Form Responses:

 - You can create workflows where actions in Excel are triggered by form responses. For example, if a respondent provides a certain answer to a form question, Power Automate can trigger a workflow that flags the response in Excel or even adds the respondent's details to a CRM system.

6. Collaboration and Sharing

Microsoft Forms and Excel allow for collaboration, enabling teams to work together on data collection and analysis:

1. Collaborating on Form Creation:

- Share your form with team members to collaborate on its design. You can grant permissions to allow others to edit the form, view responses, or both.

2. Collaborating on Data Analysis in Excel:

- Excel's sharing features allow multiple users to work on the same workbook simultaneously. This is particularly useful for teams analyzing form data together. Changes made by one user are visible to others in real-time.

3. Protecting Sensitive Data:

- Use Excel's protection features to restrict access to sensitive data. You can lock certain cells or sheets to prevent them from being edited or viewed by unauthorized users.

4. Sharing Reports:

- After analyzing your data, you can share your Excel workbook with stakeholders. Excel provides several sharing options, including sharing via email, OneDrive, or SharePoint. You can also export your data or reports to other formats, such as PDF, for broader distribution.

7. Common Scenarios for Using Microsoft Forms and Excel Together

Here are some common scenarios where integrating Microsoft Forms with Excel can be particularly powerful:

1. Surveys and Feedback Collection:

- Collect survey responses from customers or employees and analyze the data in Excel to identify trends, satisfaction levels, or areas for improvement.

2. Quizzes and Assessments:

- Use Microsoft Forms to administer quizzes and automatically calculate scores in Excel. Analyze quiz results to assess knowledge gaps or training effectiveness.

3. Event Registration and Attendance Tracking:

- Use Forms to collect event registrations and track attendance. Excel can be used to manage and analyze attendee data, helping you plan better future events.

4. Customer Support and Incident Tracking:

- Create a form for reporting customer issues or incidents. Use Excel to track, prioritize, and analyze these issues, ensuring timely resolution and identifying recurring problems.

5. Employee Timesheets:

- Collect employee timesheet data through a form and use Excel to calculate total hours worked, overtime, and more. Automate payroll calculations or integrate the data with other HR systems.

8. Troubleshooting Integration Issues

While the integration between Microsoft Forms and Excel is generally seamless, you may encounter some issues. Here's how to address common problems:

1. Data Not Updating in Excel:

- Ensure that your form is properly linked to Excel. If data is not updating automatically, try refreshing the Excel workbook or re-exporting the data from Microsoft Forms.

2. Incorrect Data Formatting:

- Sometimes, data from Forms may appear incorrectly formatted in Excel (e.g., dates appearing as text). Use Excel's built-in formatting tools to correct these issues, or apply formulas to convert data to the correct format.

3. Missing Responses:

- If some responses are missing, check the settings in Microsoft Forms to ensure that all responses are being recorded. You may also need to manually refresh the data in Excel.

4. Performance Issues with Large Datasets:

- If your form has received a large number of responses, Excel may slow down or become unresponsive. To improve performance, consider splitting the data into multiple sheets or workbooks, or using Excel's data model feature to manage large datasets.

By effectively integrating Microsoft Forms with Excel, you can unlock powerful data collection and analysis capabilities, enabling you to make better decisions and streamline your workflow. This integration is a key part of leveraging the full potential of the Microsoft 365 ecosystem for your organization's needs.

6.2.2 Forms and SharePoint

Introduction to Forms and SharePoint Integration

Microsoft Forms and SharePoint are powerful tools within the Microsoft 365 ecosystem, each offering unique features that can be significantly enhanced when used together. Microsoft Forms provides an easy-to-use platform for creating surveys, quizzes, and polls, while SharePoint offers robust capabilities for content management, collaboration, and document storage. Integrating Forms with SharePoint allows organizations to streamline workflows, centralize data collection, and enhance collaboration across teams.

This section will guide you through the process of integrating Microsoft Forms with SharePoint, from basic setup to advanced use cases. Whether you are looking to embed a form on a SharePoint page, automatically store form responses in a SharePoint list, or trigger workflows based on form submissions, this comprehensive guide will help you leverage the full potential of these tools.

Benefits of Integrating Microsoft Forms with SharePoint

Before diving into the technical steps, it's important to understand the key benefits of integrating Microsoft Forms with SharePoint:

1. Centralized Data Collection: Integrating Forms with SharePoint allows you to centralize form responses within your SharePoint environment. This makes it easier to manage, analyze, and share data across your organization.

2. Automated Workflows: With SharePoint's workflow capabilities, you can automate processes based on form submissions. For example, when a form is submitted, a new item can be automatically created in a SharePoint list, or an approval workflow can be triggered.

3. Enhanced Collaboration: By embedding Forms in SharePoint pages or sites, teams can easily access and fill out forms directly within their workspace, improving collaboration and ensuring everyone is on the same page.

4. Document Management: SharePoint's document management features allow you to link form submissions to specific documents or store attachments submitted through forms in a structured manner.

5. Secure Data Storage: SharePoint offers robust security and compliance features, ensuring that data collected through Forms is securely stored and managed according to your organization's policies.

Step-by-Step Guide to Integrating Forms with SharePoint

1. Embedding Microsoft Forms in SharePoint Pages

One of the simplest ways to integrate Microsoft Forms with SharePoint is by embedding forms directly onto SharePoint pages. This allows users to fill out forms without leaving the SharePoint environment, providing a seamless user experience.

Steps to Embed a Form in a SharePoint Page:

1. Create or Select Your Form:

   - Open Microsoft Forms and either create a new form or select an existing one.

   - Ensure the form is set up with all the required questions and settings.

2. Get the Embed Code:

   - In Microsoft Forms, navigate to the form you want to embed.

   - Click on the "Share" button in the upper right corner.

   - Select the "<>" (embed) icon to generate the embed code.

   - Copy the generated code to your clipboard.

3. Add the Embed Code to a SharePoint Page:

   - Go to your SharePoint site and navigate to the page where you want to embed the form.

- Click "Edit" on the page to enter the editing mode.

- Add a new web part by clicking the "+" sign, and search for the "Embed" web part.

- Paste the embed code into the web part's code box.

- Save and publish the page.

4. Customize the Embedded Form:

- After embedding, you can adjust the size and appearance of the form within the SharePoint page to ensure it fits well with the overall layout.

- Test the form to ensure it works correctly and is accessible to your intended audience.

2. Storing Form Responses in a SharePoint List

Another powerful integration between Microsoft Forms and SharePoint is the ability to automatically store form responses in a SharePoint list. This method is particularly useful for scenarios where you need to organize and manipulate data collected through forms, such as in task tracking, project management, or issue logging.

Steps to Store Form Responses in a SharePoint List:

1. Create a SharePoint List:

- Go to your SharePoint site and create a new list.

- Define the columns in the list that correspond to the questions in your Microsoft Form. For example, if your form has fields for "Name," "Email," and "Feedback," create matching columns in your SharePoint list.

- Ensure that the column types in the SharePoint list match the data types in the form (e.g., text, number, date).

2. Connect Microsoft Forms to SharePoint Using Power Automate:

- Open Power Automate (formerly known as Microsoft Flow) from your Microsoft 365 account.

- Create a new flow by selecting "Automated flow" and choosing "When a new response is submitted" as the trigger.

- Select the Microsoft Form that you want to connect.

- Add an action to the flow: "Get response details." This action retrieves the details of the form submission.

3. Map Form Responses to SharePoint List Columns:

- Add another action to the flow: "Create item."

- Select your SharePoint site and list.

- Map the form fields to the corresponding columns in the SharePoint list. For example, map the "Name" field from the form to the "Name" column in the SharePoint list.

- Save the flow.

4. Test the Flow:

- Submit a test response through the form.

- Check the SharePoint list to verify that the response has been correctly added as a new item.

- Adjust the flow if necessary to ensure data is captured accurately.

3. Creating Automated Workflows with SharePoint and Forms

One of the most powerful aspects of integrating Forms with SharePoint is the ability to create automated workflows. This can significantly reduce manual effort and improve efficiency in processes such as approvals, notifications, and task assignments.

Example: Approval Workflow for Form Submissions:

1. Design the Approval Workflow:

- Define the workflow process. For example, when a form is submitted, an approval request should be sent to a manager. If approved, an item is created in a SharePoint list; if rejected, the submitter is notified.

2. Set Up the Workflow in Power Automate:

   - Start by creating a new flow in Power Automate.

   - Trigger the flow when a new response is submitted to the form.

   - Use the "Get response details" action to capture the form submission data.

   - Add the "Start and wait for an approval" action, where you can configure the approval details, including the approver and the message.

3. Conditionally Create SharePoint List Items:

   - Add a condition to the flow to check if the submission was approved.

   - If the submission is approved, use the "Create item" action to add a new item to a SharePoint list.

   - If the submission is rejected, use the "Send an email" action to notify the submitter of the rejection and any next steps.

4. Test and Refine the Workflow:

   - Run tests to ensure the workflow functions as expected.

   - Make adjustments as needed, such as customizing the approval messages or adding additional steps to the workflow.

4. Handling Attachments in Forms and SharePoint

If your Microsoft Form includes file upload questions, you can configure SharePoint to automatically store these attachments. This ensures that all documents or files submitted through the form are securely stored and easily accessible within SharePoint.

Steps to Store Form Attachments in SharePoint:

1. Configure the File Upload Question:

   - In Microsoft Forms, add a "File Upload" question to your form.

   - Specify the number of files allowed, file size limits, and accepted file types.

2. Set Up a Flow in Power Automate to Handle Attachments:

- Create a new flow triggered by a new form submission.

- Use the "Get response details" action to retrieve submission details.

- Use the "Get file content" action to retrieve the uploaded file(s).

3. Store Files in a SharePoint Document Library:

- Add the "Create file" action to the flow, specifying the SharePoint site and document library where the file should be stored.

- Map the file content from the form to the SharePoint library.

4. Link Attachments to SharePoint List Items:

- If storing both form responses and attachments, consider adding a hyperlink or attachment field to your SharePoint list item that links directly to the file stored in the document library.

5. Test and Validate File Handling:

- Submit a test form with attachments to ensure that files are correctly uploaded and stored in SharePoint.

- Verify that links to attachments are correctly created in SharePoint list items.

Best Practices for Integrating Forms with SharePoint

To ensure a successful integration of Microsoft Forms with SharePoint, consider the following best practices:

1. Consistent Naming Conventions:

- Use clear and consistent naming conventions for forms, SharePoint lists, and Power Automate flows to avoid confusion and maintain organization.

2. Security and Permissions:

- Ensure that appropriate permissions are set up in SharePoint to control who can view, edit, and manage form responses and attachments.

- Regularly review permissions to ensure data security.

3. Testing and Quality Assurance:

- Thoroughly test all integrations, workflows, and form setups before rolling them out to a larger audience.

- Involve stakeholders in testing to gather feedback and identify potential issues.

4. Documentation and Training:

- Document the integration process, including how forms are connected to SharePoint and how workflows are configured.

- Provide training to team members on how to use the integrated system effectively.

5. Monitoring and Maintenance:

- Regularly monitor the performance of your integrated system, including checking for any issues with data synchronization or workflow execution.

- Update forms, SharePoint lists, and workflows as needed to reflect changes in processes or requirements.

Conclusion

Integrating Microsoft Forms with SharePoint offers a powerful way to enhance data collection, streamline workflows, and improve collaboration within your organization. Whether you are embedding forms on SharePoint pages, storing responses in SharePoint lists, or creating complex workflows, this integration can greatly improve the efficiency and effectiveness of your business processes. By following the detailed steps and best practices outlined in this section, you can ensure a smooth and successful integration that meets your organization's needs.

6.3 Third-Party Integrations

Third-party integrations extend the functionality of Microsoft Forms, allowing users to automate workflows, connect with other apps, and enhance data management capabilities. One of the most powerful tools for integrating Microsoft Forms with other services is Zapier. In this section, we'll delve into how to use Zapier with Microsoft Forms to streamline processes and create automated workflows.

6.3.1 Using Zapier with Microsoft Forms

Introduction to Zapier

Zapier is a popular automation tool that connects different apps and services without requiring any coding skills. It enables you to create "Zaps," which are automated workflows that link two or more apps to perform a specific task. For example, you could create a Zap that automatically sends form responses to a Google Sheet, sends an email notification, or triggers an event in another app whenever someone submits a form in Microsoft Forms.

Setting Up a Zapier Account

Before integrating Microsoft Forms with Zapier, you need to set up a Zapier account. If you don't already have an account, follow these steps:

1. Sign Up for Zapier:

   - Visit the [Zapier website](https://zapier.com/) and click on the "Sign Up" button.

   - You can sign up using your email address, Google account, or Microsoft account.

   - Follow the on-screen instructions to complete the registration process.

2. Choose a Plan:

   - Zapier offers several pricing plans, including a free plan that allows you to create up to five Zaps with limited features.

- If you need more advanced features or a higher number of Zaps, consider choosing a paid plan that suits your needs.

3. Familiarize Yourself with the Zapier Dashboard:

  - Once you're logged in, you'll be directed to the Zapier dashboard.

  - The dashboard is where you can create, manage, and monitor your Zaps.

  - Take a moment to explore the interface, including the options for creating new Zaps and viewing existing ones.

Connecting Microsoft Forms to Zapier

Now that your Zapier account is set up, the next step is to connect Microsoft Forms to Zapier. This connection allows Zapier to access your form data and use it as a trigger for various actions. Here's how to do it:

1. Create a New Zap:

  - On the Zapier dashboard, click on the "Make a Zap" button to start creating a new Zap.

  - You'll be guided through a step-by-step process to set up your Zap.

2. Choose a Trigger App:

  - In the "Choose App & Event" section, search for "Microsoft Forms" and select it as your trigger app.

  - If this is your first time connecting Microsoft Forms to Zapier, you'll be prompted to sign in to your Microsoft account.

  - After signing in, grant Zapier permission to access your Microsoft Forms account.

3. Select a Trigger Event:

  - After connecting Microsoft Forms, you'll need to choose a trigger event. The most common trigger event is "New Response in Form," which activates the Zap whenever someone submits a new response to your form.

  - Select this trigger event and click "Continue."

4. Choose the Form:

  - Zapier will prompt you to select the specific form you want to use for this Zap.

  - Choose the form from the dropdown list and click "Continue."

5. Test the Trigger:

  - Zapier will test the connection to ensure it's working correctly. It will pull in recent form responses to verify that the integration is set up correctly.

  - If the test is successful, you'll see a sample response that you can use to set up the rest of the Zap.

Defining Actions with Zapier

Once the trigger is set up, the next step is to define the action(s) that will occur when the trigger event happens. Zapier offers a wide range of apps and services that you can connect to Microsoft Forms. Below are some common use cases:

1. Sending Form Responses to Google Sheets:

  - If you want to store form responses in a Google Sheet for easy data management and analysis, you can set up a Zap to do this automatically.

  - In the "Action" section of the Zap, search for "Google Sheets" and select it as your action app.

  - Choose the action event "Create Spreadsheet Row" and connect your Google account to Zapier.

  - Select the Google Sheet and worksheet where you want the data to be added.

  - Map the form fields from Microsoft Forms to the corresponding columns in your Google Sheet.

2. Sending Email Notifications:

  - You can set up a Zap to send an email notification whenever a new response is received.

- Choose "Email by Zapier" as the action app and select the action event "Send Outbound Email."

- Configure the email settings, including the recipient, subject, and body of the email. You can include form response data in the email body by mapping the form fields.

3. Creating a Task in Trello:

- If you're using Trello for project management, you can create a Zap that automatically adds a task (card) to a Trello board based on form responses.

- Select "Trello" as the action app and choose the action event "Create Card."

- Connect your Trello account, select the board and list where you want the card to be created, and map the form responses to the card's title, description, and other fields.

4. Posting to Slack:

- For teams that use Slack for communication, you can create a Zap that posts a message to a Slack channel whenever a new form response is received.

- Choose "Slack" as the action app and select the action event "Send Channel Message."

- Connect your Slack account, choose the channel where you want to post the message, and customize the message content with form response data.

5. Adding Contacts to a CRM:

- If you're collecting customer information through Microsoft Forms, you can automatically add new contacts to your CRM (e.g., Salesforce, HubSpot) using a Zap.

- Select your CRM as the action app and choose the appropriate action event (e.g., "Create Contact").

- Connect your CRM account, and map the form fields to the corresponding contact fields in your CRM.

Testing and Activating Your Zap

After setting up the trigger and action(s), it's crucial to test your Zap to ensure everything works as expected. Zapier allows you to test the entire workflow before activating it:

1. Test the Zap:

 - Zapier will run a test using the sample data from the trigger step.

 - Review the results to ensure that the actions are performed correctly.

 - If any issues are detected, Zapier will provide error messages or suggestions for troubleshooting.

2. Activate the Zap:

 - Once the test is successful, you can activate the Zap by clicking the "Turn on Zap" button.

 - Your Zap is now live and will automatically perform the defined actions whenever the trigger event occurs.

Managing and Monitoring Your Zaps

After your Zap is activated, you can manage and monitor its performance from the Zapier dashboard:

1. View Zap History:

 - Zapier keeps a log of all the times your Zaps have run. You can view the history to see when each Zap was triggered and whether the actions were completed successfully.

 - The history includes detailed logs of each step in the Zap, making it easier to troubleshoot any issues.

2. Edit or Update Zaps:

 - You can edit existing Zaps at any time to change the trigger, action, or settings.

 - If your form or workflow changes, update the Zap to reflect the new requirements.

3. Turn Zaps On or Off:

 - You can temporarily disable a Zap without deleting it by toggling the switch next to the Zap's name on the dashboard.

 - This is useful if you want to pause a workflow or make updates without immediately affecting live data.

4. Clone or Share Zaps:

- Zapier allows you to clone existing Zaps if you want to create similar workflows with minor modifications.

- You can also share Zaps with others by generating a sharing link or exporting the Zap settings.

Advanced Zapier Techniques

For those who want to take their Zapier workflows to the next level, there are several advanced techniques you can explore:

1. Multi-Step Zaps:

- Instead of just one action, you can set up Zaps with multiple steps, allowing for more complex workflows.

- For example, you could create a Zap that adds a new contact to your CRM, sends an email notification, and updates a Google Sheet—all from a single form submission.

2. Conditional Logic with Paths:

- Zapier offers a feature called "Paths" that allows you to create conditional logic in your Zaps.

- With Paths, you can set different actions based on certain conditions. For example, if a respondent selects "Yes" on a form question, the Zap could follow one path, while selecting "No" could trigger a different set of actions.

3. Delays and Scheduling:

- You can add delays to your Zaps, allowing you to wait a certain amount of time before performing an action.

- This is useful for scenarios where you want to space out tasks or schedule actions for a specific time.

4. Using Filters:

- Filters allow you to control when your Zaps run based on specific criteria.

- For instance, you might only want a Zap to run if a form response includes a certain keyword or if a particular checkbox is selected.

Conclusion

Integrating Microsoft Forms with Zapier opens up a world of possibilities for automating your workflows and making data management more efficient. Whether you're sending form responses to other apps, creating tasks in project management tools, or setting up complex multi-step workflows, Zapier provides the flexibility and power to enhance your Microsoft Forms experience. By leveraging these integrations, you can save time, reduce manual work, and ensure that your form data is used effectively across your organization.

6.3.2 Other Useful Integrations

Integrating Microsoft Forms with third-party tools can significantly enhance its functionality, allowing you to automate workflows, analyze data more effectively, and extend the capabilities of your forms. While Zapier is one of the most popular tools for integrating Microsoft Forms with other applications, there are several other integrations that can be equally powerful depending on your needs. In this section, we'll explore some of these useful integrations, including their benefits, setup processes, and practical applications.

1. Microsoft Power Automate

Overview:

Microsoft Power Automate (formerly known as Microsoft Flow) is a robust automation tool that allows users to create automated workflows between various apps and services. By integrating Microsoft Forms with Power Automate, you can automate repetitive tasks, such as sending notifications, saving responses to a database, or triggering actions in other applications when a form is submitted.

Benefits:

- Automation of Repetitive Tasks: Save time by automating tasks like data entry, notifications, and follow-up emails.

- Enhanced Workflow Efficiency: Streamline processes across different applications without manual intervention.

- Customizable Workflows: Tailor workflows to fit specific business needs or processes.

Setting Up the Integration:

1. Access Power Automate: Log in to your Microsoft account and navigate to [Power Automate](https://flow.microsoft.com/).

2. Create a New Flow: Click on "Create" and select "Automated cloud flow" to start a new workflow.

3. Select a Trigger: Choose "When a new response is submitted" as the trigger for your flow. This ensures that the flow begins whenever someone completes your form.

4. Add Actions: After selecting the trigger, you can add various actions to your flow. For example, you might choose to:

   - Send an email notification to a specific person or group.

   - Save the form responses to an Excel file or SharePoint list.

   - Trigger an approval process in Microsoft Teams.

5. Test and Save Your Flow: Before going live, test your flow to ensure it works as expected. Once verified, save the flow, and it will automatically execute whenever the form is submitted.

Practical Applications:

- Event Registration: Automatically send a confirmation email to participants after they register for an event via Microsoft Forms.

- Customer Support: Log support requests from forms directly into a ticketing system like Zendesk.

- Employee Surveys: Send survey results directly to a manager's email or a dedicated HR folder for further analysis.

2. Microsoft Power BI

Overview:

Microsoft Power BI is a business analytics service that provides interactive visualizations and business intelligence capabilities. Integrating Microsoft Forms with Power BI allows you to visualize and analyze form responses in real-time, offering deeper insights into the data collected.

Benefits:

- Real-Time Data Visualization: View form responses as they come in, with dynamic charts and graphs.

- Advanced Data Analysis: Use Power BI's robust analytical tools to identify trends, patterns, and correlations within your data.

- Custom Dashboards: Create tailored dashboards that display the most relevant information for your needs.

Setting Up the Integration:

1. Prepare Your Form Data: Ensure that your Microsoft Forms responses are being saved to an Excel file stored in OneDrive or SharePoint.

2. Access Power BI: Log in to [Power BI](https://powerbi.microsoft.com/) with your Microsoft account.

3. Connect to Your Data Source: In Power BI, select "Get Data" and choose "OneDrive" or "SharePoint" as your data source. Locate and connect to the Excel file containing your form responses.

4. Create Visualizations: Once connected, you can start building visualizations. Choose from a variety of charts, graphs, and tables to represent your data.

5. Build Dashboards: Combine multiple visualizations into a single dashboard to monitor key metrics and insights in real time.

Practical Applications:

- Customer Feedback Analysis: Analyze customer satisfaction scores from survey responses to identify areas for improvement.

- Employee Engagement: Visualize employee feedback from internal surveys to track engagement over time.

- Market Research: Use forms to collect market data and analyze responses to make informed business decisions.

3. Google Sheets

Overview:

While Microsoft Forms integrates seamlessly with Excel, some users prefer to work with Google Sheets, especially if they use other Google Workspace tools. By using Zapier or similar automation tools, you can automatically transfer form responses to a Google Sheets spreadsheet.

Benefits:

- Cross-Platform Data Management: Manage data in Google Sheets while collecting responses through Microsoft Forms.

- Collaborative Data Sharing: Easily share and collaborate on form data with colleagues who use Google Workspace.

- Real-Time Data Syncing: Automatically sync new responses to Google Sheets as they come in.

Setting Up the Integration:

1. Use Zapier: As of now, there is no direct integration between Microsoft Forms and Google Sheets. However, you can use Zapier to create a "Zap" that automatically sends form responses to a Google Sheets file.

2. Set Up the Trigger: In Zapier, choose "Microsoft Forms" as the trigger app and select "New Response" as the trigger event.

3. Choose the Action: Select "Google Sheets" as the action app and "Create Spreadsheet Row" as the action event. Connect your Google account and choose the specific Google Sheets file where you want the data to be saved.

4. Map the Fields: Match the form fields to the corresponding columns in your Google Sheets.

5. Test and Activate the Zap: Test the Zap to ensure that the data is being correctly transferred from Microsoft Forms to Google Sheets. Once confirmed, activate the Zap.

Practical Applications:

- Project Management: Track project progress and update statuses in Google Sheets based on team input collected through Microsoft Forms.

- Data Backup: Maintain a backup of all form responses in Google Sheets for redundancy.

- Collaboration: Collaborate with team members who prefer using Google Workspace for data analysis.

4. Trello

Overview:

Trello is a popular project management tool that uses boards, lists, and cards to help teams organize and prioritize tasks. Integrating Microsoft Forms with Trello allows you to automatically create Trello cards based on form responses, streamlining task management and delegation.

Benefits:

- Automated Task Creation: Automatically generate Trello cards when a form is submitted, reducing manual data entry.

- Improved Workflow Efficiency: Ensure that tasks and issues are tracked and managed promptly.

- Customizable Workflows: Tailor the integration to fit the specific needs of your project or team.

Setting Up the Integration:

1. Use Zapier or Power Automate: Both Zapier and Microsoft Power Automate can be used to create the integration between Microsoft Forms and Trello.

2. Set Up the Trigger: Choose "Microsoft Forms" as the trigger app and "New Response" as the trigger event.

3. Choose the Action: Select "Trello" as the action app and "Create Card" as the action event. Connect your Trello account and specify the board and list where new cards should be created.

4. Map the Fields: Map the form fields to the corresponding fields in Trello, such as the card title, description, and due date.

5. Test and Activate the Workflow: Test the integration to ensure that Trello cards are being created as expected. Once confirmed, activate the workflow.

Practical Applications:

- Issue Tracking: Automatically create Trello cards for each support issue reported via Microsoft Forms.

- Task Management: Use forms to collect project updates and generate corresponding Trello tasks.

- Event Planning: Streamline event planning by generating tasks and checklists in Trello based on responses from an event registration form.

5. Slack

Overview:

Slack is a messaging app for teams that integrates with numerous tools and services. By integrating Microsoft Forms with Slack, you can receive instant notifications or updates in a Slack channel whenever a form is submitted, keeping your team informed in real-time.

Benefits:

- Instant Notifications: Receive immediate alerts in Slack when a new form response is submitted.

- Enhanced Team Collaboration: Keep your team updated on form submissions without needing to manually check responses.

- Custom Alerts: Customize the alerts to include specific form data or trigger specific actions within Slack.

Setting Up the Integration:

1. Use Zapier or Power Automate: You can use either of these tools to create the integration between Microsoft Forms and Slack.

2. Set Up the Trigger: Choose "Microsoft Forms" as the trigger app and "New Response" as the trigger event.

3. Choose the Action: Select "Slack" as the action app and "Send Channel Message" or "Send Direct Message" as the action event. Connect your Slack account and specify the channel or user to receive the notifications.

4. Customize the Message: Personalize the message to include relevant details from the form, such as the respondent's name or specific answers.

5. Test and Activate the Workflow: Test the workflow to ensure that Slack notifications are being sent as expected. Once confirmed, activate the workflow.

Practical Applications:

- Customer Feedback: Notify your customer support team immediately when feedback is submitted through a form.

- Incident Reporting: Automatically alert your IT team in Slack when a system issue is reported via a form.

- Team Surveys: Share survey results in a specific Slack channel for team-wide discussion.

6. Mailchimp

Overview:

Mailchimp is a widely used email marketing platform. By integrating Microsoft Forms with Mailchimp, you can automatically add respondents to your email lists, send follow-up emails, or trigger email campaigns based on form submissions.

Benefits:

- Automated Email Campaigns: Automatically enroll respondents in email campaigns based on their form submissions.

- Streamlined Marketing Workflows: Reduce the need for manual data entry and ensure that your email lists are always up-to-date.

- Targeted Marketing: Use form responses to segment your audience and send personalized email content.

Setting Up the Integration:

1. Use Zapier: Since there is no direct integration between Microsoft Forms and Mailchimp, Zapier can be used to bridge the gap.

2. Set Up the Trigger: Choose "Microsoft Forms" as the trigger app and "New Response" as the trigger event.

3. Choose the Action: Select "Mailchimp" as the action app and "Add/Update Subscriber" as the action event. Connect your Mailchimp account and specify the email list to add respondents to.

4. Map the Fields: Match the form fields to the corresponding fields in Mailchimp, such as email address, name, and other relevant data.

5. Test and Activate the Workflow: Test the integration to ensure that respondents are being correctly added to your Mailchimp list. Once confirmed, activate the workflow.

Practical Applications:

- Newsletter Subscriptions: Automatically add respondents who opt-in via a form to your newsletter mailing list.

- Event Follow-Up: Send follow-up emails to event attendees who registered through Microsoft Forms.

- Targeted Email Campaigns: Use form data to segment your audience and send tailored email content based on their preferences or responses.

7. Salesforce

Overview:

Salesforce is a leading customer relationship management (CRM) platform. By integrating Microsoft Forms with Salesforce, you can automatically create leads, contacts, or cases based on form submissions, streamlining your sales and customer service processes.

Benefits:

- Automated Lead Generation: Instantly create leads in Salesforce when a potential customer fills out a form.

- Improved Data Accuracy: Ensure that customer information is accurately captured and entered into your CRM.

- Enhanced Sales Workflows: Streamline the sales process by reducing manual data entry and ensuring timely follow-up.

Setting Up the Integration:

1. Use Zapier or Power Automate: Both tools can be used to connect Microsoft Forms with Salesforce.

2. Set Up the Trigger: Choose "Microsoft Forms" as the trigger app and "New Response" as the trigger event.

3. Choose the Action: Select "Salesforce" as the action app and "Create Record" as the action event. Connect your Salesforce account and specify the type of record to create (e.g., Lead, Contact, Case).

4. Map the Fields: Map the form fields to the corresponding fields in Salesforce, such as the lead's name, email, and phone number.

5. Test and Activate the Workflow: Test the integration to ensure that records are being correctly created in Salesforce. Once confirmed, activate the workflow.

Practical Applications:

- Lead Capture: Automatically create new leads in Salesforce from potential customers who fill out a contact form on your website.

- Customer Support: Generate support cases in Salesforce from customer feedback or issue reports submitted via Microsoft Forms.

- Sales Follow-Up: Ensure that your sales team receives instant notifications when a new lead is created, enabling timely follow-up.

Conclusion:

Integrating Microsoft Forms with third-party tools can unlock a wealth of possibilities, enhancing the functionality and efficiency of your forms. Whether you're looking to automate workflows, analyze data, manage projects, or improve customer engagement, these integrations provide the flexibility and power needed to achieve your goals. By leveraging the capabilities of tools like Power Automate, Power BI, Google Sheets, Trello, Slack, Mailchimp, and Salesforce, you can create a seamless and efficient system that maximizes the value of the data collected through Microsoft Forms.

CHAPTER VII
Best Practices for Effective Forms and Quizzes

7.1 Designing Engaging Forms

Creating a form that is engaging, effective, and easy to understand is critical to collecting quality data. Whether your goal is to gather feedback, conduct research, or assess knowledge through quizzes, the way you design your questions plays a pivotal role in the success of your form. In this section, we'll delve into the art and science of writing clear questions, ensuring your respondents provide meaningful and accurate answers.

7.1.1 Writing Clear Questions

Clear and concise questions are the foundation of any effective form or quiz. Poorly worded questions can lead to confusion, misinterpretation, and ultimately, unreliable data. To write questions that are easy to understand and answer, consider the following guidelines:

1. Use Simple Language

The first step to writing clear questions is to use simple, straightforward language. Avoid technical jargon, complex sentences, and unnecessary words that may confuse respondents. Instead, opt for plain language that is easily understood by your target audience. For instance, instead of asking, "What is your opinion on the utilization of alternative transportation modalities?" you could simply ask, "What do you think about using alternative transportation methods?"

2. Be Specific and Direct

Questions should be specific and to the point. Ambiguous or vague questions can lead to varied interpretations, resulting in data that is difficult to analyze. For example, instead of asking, "How often do you use this product?" be more specific by asking, "How many times per week do you use this product?" The latter question is more likely to yield precise and actionable responses.

3. Avoid Double-Barreled Questions

A common mistake in question design is the double-barreled question, which asks about two things at once. This can confuse respondents and lead to unclear answers. For example, a double-barreled question might be, "How satisfied are you with our product's quality and customer service?" Instead, break it down into two separate questions: "How satisfied are you with our product's quality?" and "How satisfied are you with our customer service?"

4. Provide Balanced Answer Choices

When designing multiple-choice questions, ensure that the answer choices are balanced and cover the full range of possible responses. This prevents bias and allows respondents to choose an option that best reflects their opinion or experience. For instance, if you're asking about satisfaction levels, provide a balanced scale such as: "Very satisfied," "Satisfied," "Neutral," "Dissatisfied," and "Very dissatisfied."

5. Use Neutral Wording

The wording of your questions should be neutral, without leading the respondent toward a particular answer. Leading questions can skew the data and undermine the integrity of your results. For example, a leading question might be, "How much do you enjoy our excellent customer service?" A neutral alternative would be, "How would you rate our customer service?"

6. Consider the Order of Questions

The order in which you present questions can influence how respondents perceive and answer them. Start with general questions and move towards more specific ones.

Additionally, sensitive or potentially difficult questions should be placed towards the end of the form, once the respondent has built up some rapport with the survey. For instance, begin with questions like "How often do you use our product?" before asking about satisfaction or personal opinions.

7. Use Open-Ended Questions Wisely

Open-ended questions can provide valuable insights but should be used sparingly. They require more effort from respondents and may lead to incomplete answers if the question is too broad. When using open-ended questions, be specific and guide the respondent with a clear focus. For example, instead of asking, "What do you think about our product?" you could ask, "What features of our product do you find most useful and why?"

8. Test Your Questions

Before finalizing your form, it's essential to test your questions with a small group from your target audience. This allows you to identify any potential issues with wording, clarity, or interpretation. Based on their feedback, make necessary adjustments to ensure your questions are as clear and effective as possible.

9. Avoid Negative Wording

Negative wording can confuse respondents and lead to inaccurate answers. Questions like "Do you disagree that our product is not easy to use?" are unnecessarily complicated. Instead, rephrase the question in a positive form, such as "Do you agree that our product is easy to use?"

10. Make Use of Skip Logic

Skip logic allows respondents to bypass irrelevant questions based on their previous answers. This not only streamlines the survey-taking process but also prevents confusion and frustration. For example, if a respondent indicates they do not use a particular feature of your product, skip any subsequent questions related to that feature.

11. Ensure Cultural Sensitivity

When writing questions, especially for a diverse or international audience, be mindful of cultural differences that may affect how questions are understood or answered. Avoid idioms, phrases, or references that may not translate well or might be interpreted differently in various cultures. For example, instead of using a phrase like "beating around the bush," opt for more universally understood language such as "avoiding the main point."

12. Keep Questions Focused

Each question should focus on one specific topic or idea. Overly broad questions can confuse respondents and result in less reliable data. For instance, instead of asking, "What do you think about our company?" break it down into more focused questions like "How do you feel about our product quality?" and "How would you rate our customer service?"

13. Offer a "Don't Know" or "Not Applicable" Option

For some questions, respondents might not have an opinion or the question might not apply to them. In these cases, it's helpful to include a "Don't Know" or "Not Applicable" option. This allows respondents to skip questions that they cannot answer accurately, leading to more reliable data overall.

14. Be Mindful of Survey Fatigue

Survey fatigue can occur when respondents are overwhelmed by the length or complexity of a survey, leading to rushed or incomplete responses. To combat this, keep your questions concise and relevant, and avoid unnecessary repetition. Additionally, consider the overall length of your survey and the time it will take to complete.

15. Review and Revise

Finally, take the time to review and revise your questions. A fresh look can help you catch any unclear wording, biases, or errors that may have been overlooked. It's also beneficial to have a colleague or someone unfamiliar with the survey content review the questions to ensure they are clear and understandable.

Practical Example of Writing Clear Questions

Let's apply these guidelines to an example scenario where you're creating a survey to assess customer satisfaction with a software product.

Initial Question:

"How satisfied are you with our software?"

Revised Question Following Guidelines:

- Specificity: "How satisfied are you with the performance of our software in terms of speed and reliability?"

- Simple Language: "How easy is it for you to navigate our software?"

- Avoid Double-Barreled: Instead of asking, "How satisfied are you with the software and our customer support?" break it down into: "How satisfied are you with our software?" and "How satisfied are you with our customer support?"

Balanced Answer Choices Example:

"How would you rate the ease of use of our software?"

- Very easy to use

- Easy to use

- Neutral

- Difficult to use

- Very difficult to use

Neutral Wording Example:

Instead of "Do you agree that our software is the best on the market?" consider asking "How would you rate our software compared to other similar products?"

Cultural Sensitivity Example:

Instead of asking, "Do you find our software a home run?" ask "Do you find our software highly successful?"

By implementing these strategies, your forms and quizzes will be more engaging, clearer, and better structured to elicit meaningful responses, ultimately leading to more actionable insights.

7.1.2 Keeping Forms Concise

Introduction

In an age where attention spans are shorter than ever, creating concise forms is crucial for maintaining user engagement. A well-structured, concise form not only respects the respondent's time but also increases the likelihood of receiving thoughtful, complete responses. In this section, we will delve into the strategies and best practices for keeping your forms concise while still gathering the necessary data.

Why Conciseness Matters

Conciseness in form design is essential for several reasons:

1. Improved Completion Rates: Respondents are more likely to complete shorter forms. A lengthy form can overwhelm users, leading to abandonment.

2. Enhanced User Experience: Concise forms create a positive experience by making the process quick and straightforward, which reflects well on your brand or organization.

3. Better Data Quality: By focusing on essential questions, you reduce the risk of respondents providing inaccurate or rushed answers just to finish the form.

Strategies for Keeping Forms Concise

To keep your forms concise, consider the following strategies:

1. Define Clear Objectives

Before creating your form, clearly define what information you need to collect. Every question should serve a specific purpose aligned with your objectives. If a question doesn't directly contribute to your goals, consider omitting it.

- Ask Yourself: What is the primary goal of this form? What information is essential to achieve this goal?

- Prioritize Questions: Rank your questions by importance, and consider eliminating or combining lower-priority questions.

2. Use Simple, Direct Language

Write questions and instructions in a clear, straightforward manner. Avoid jargon or complex phrasing that might confuse respondents or require additional explanations.

- Keep It Short: Use as few words as possible to convey your message. For example, instead of asking, "Can you please describe your level of satisfaction with our service?" you might ask, "How satisfied are you with our service?"

- Be Specific: Vague questions can lead to vague answers. Be specific to avoid ambiguity and ensure you get the information you need.

3. Limit the Number of Questions

The fewer questions you ask, the more likely respondents are to complete the form. Consider the following approaches:

- Combine Questions: Where possible, combine related questions into a single query. For example, instead of asking "How satisfied are you with our service?" and "How likely are you to recommend us?" consider combining them into one question with a scale that covers both aspects.

- Skip Logic: Use skip logic to only show questions that are relevant to the respondent. This reduces the total number of questions each respondent sees, making the form feel shorter.

4. Focus on Essential Information

It can be tempting to gather as much information as possible, but this often leads to bloated forms. Focus on the essentials by:

- Eliminating Redundancies: Review your form for redundant questions or those that overlap in purpose.

- Optional Questions: If you must ask additional questions, make them optional. This allows respondents to skip non-essential questions if they wish.

5. Group Related Questions

Organizing your form into sections with related questions can make it easier for respondents to navigate and understand. This also helps you maintain a logical flow, reducing the need for unnecessary questions.

- Use Sections: Break your form into sections, each focused on a specific topic. This not only improves clarity but also gives the form a natural rhythm, making it easier to follow.

- Review Each Section: After creating each section, review it to ensure that every question is necessary and contributes to your form's overall objective.

6. Leverage Question Types Effectively

Different question types can help streamline your form and make it more concise:

- Multiple Choice and Rating Scales: These question types allow respondents to quickly select an answer, reducing the time and effort required to complete the form.

- Dropdown Menus: Use dropdown menus to save space and keep the form visually clean, especially when offering many options.

- Yes/No Questions: These are quick to answer and can simplify the decision-making process for respondents.

7. Use Pre-Filled Data When Possible

If you already have information about your respondents, pre-fill certain fields to save them time. For example, if you know the respondent's name and email, pre-fill these fields so they don't have to.

- Automated Forms: Consider using forms that can automatically pull in data from your database or CRM, reducing the number of questions the respondent needs to answer manually.

- Validation: Ensure pre-filled data is accurate and relevant to avoid any confusion or frustration.

8. Test and Refine Your Form

Testing your form is an essential step in ensuring conciseness:

- Pilot Testing: Before launching, test your form with a small group. Ask for feedback on the length and clarity, and make adjustments based on their input.

- Analyze Drop-Off Rates: After your form is live, monitor where respondents are dropping off. High drop-off rates at certain questions may indicate that they are too complex or unnecessary.

9. Use Visual Cues for Brevity

Visual design plays a significant role in how long a form feels. Even a short form can seem long if it's poorly designed. Consider these tips:

- Whitespace: Use whitespace strategically to create a clean and uncluttered look. This makes the form feel shorter and more approachable.

- Progress Bars: If your form has multiple sections, include a progress bar to show respondents how much is left. This can motivate them to complete the form, even if it's longer.

- Short Sentences and Bullet Points: Break down information into bullet points or short sentences to improve readability and make the form appear less dense.

Examples of Concise Forms

1. Customer Feedback Form:

 - This form asks for a rating of the service, a short comment, and whether the customer would recommend the service. It's brief and to the point, ensuring high completion rates.

2. Event Registration Form:

 - A simple form that asks for the attendee's name, contact information, and session preferences. It avoids unnecessary questions about dietary restrictions unless the event includes a meal.

3. Employee Satisfaction Survey:

 - Focuses on key areas such as work environment, management, and professional development. Optional comments sections allow for additional feedback without overwhelming the respondent.

Conclusion

Keeping your forms concise is a balance between gathering the necessary data and respecting your respondents' time. By defining clear objectives, using simple language, and focusing on essential information, you can create forms that are not only engaging but also effective in collecting high-quality data. Remember, the goal is to make the process as easy and efficient as possible for your respondents, which in turn will result in better completion rates and more reliable data.

7.2 Increasing Response Rates

Ensuring a high response rate is crucial for the success of your survey or quiz. Without a sufficient number of responses, the data collected may not be representative, making it difficult to draw meaningful conclusions. This section will explore effective strategies for distributing your forms to maximize response rates.

7.2.1 Effective Distribution Strategies

Choosing the right distribution strategies can make a significant difference in how many people complete your survey or quiz. The key is to meet your audience where they are and to make the process as convenient as possible for them. Below are several proven strategies to effectively distribute your Microsoft Forms:

1. Direct Email Invitations

One of the most direct and effective ways to distribute your form is through email. Sending a personalized email invitation can significantly boost your response rates. Here's how to do it effectively:

- Personalization: Address the recipient by name and customize the email content to make it relevant to them. Mention why their participation is valuable and how their feedback will be used.

- Clear Call to Action: Ensure that the email contains a clear and prominent link to the form. Use action-oriented language such as "Click here to complete the survey" to encourage participation.

- Timing: Send your email at a time when your audience is most likely to be available to respond. Research suggests that mid-week and mid-morning are optimal times for sending survey invitations.

- Follow-up Reminders: If recipients don't respond within a few days, send a polite reminder email. Be sure to express appreciation for their time and reiterate the importance of their input.

2. Embedding Forms in Websites and Blogs

Embedding your form directly into a website or blog can increase visibility and make it easy for visitors to participate without leaving the page. Here's how to do it:

- Relevant Content Placement: Embed the form on a webpage that is relevant to the survey content. For instance, if you're surveying customer satisfaction, place the form on a thank-you page or a customer feedback section.

- Responsive Design: Ensure that the embedded form is responsive and works well on all devices, including mobile phones and tablets. Microsoft Forms are inherently responsive, but it's always good to test the embedded form across various devices.

- Visibility: Place the form in a visible location on the page, preferably above the fold, so visitors don't need to scroll down to find it.

3. Sharing on Social Media

Social media platforms are powerful tools for distributing your form to a broader audience. Here's how to use them effectively:

- Platform Selection: Choose the social media platforms where your target audience is most active. For professional surveys, LinkedIn may be more appropriate, whereas Facebook or Twitter might be better for general audiences.

- Engaging Posts: Create posts that grab attention. Use compelling headlines, visuals, and a brief explanation of the survey's purpose. Don't forget to include a clear call-to-action link to the form.

- Hashtags and Targeting: Use relevant hashtags to increase the reach of your posts. On platforms like Facebook, you can also use paid targeting to reach specific demographics.

- Groups and Communities: Share the form in relevant groups or communities. For example, if you're conducting a survey on education, post it in education-focused groups on LinkedIn or Facebook.

4. Leveraging Microsoft Teams and Other Collaboration Tools

If your audience includes colleagues, students, or any group you work with regularly, using collaboration tools like Microsoft Teams can be highly effective:

- Integration with Teams: Microsoft Forms integrates seamlessly with Teams, allowing you to create and share forms directly within a team or channel. This is particularly useful for workplace surveys or quizzes in educational settings.

- Announcements: Use the announcements feature in Teams to draw attention to the form. You can pin the form to a channel or set it as a priority notification.

- Regular Reminders: Post reminders in the relevant channels, especially if the form is time-sensitive. Encourage team members to complete the form during a scheduled meeting or break.

5. QR Codes for Offline Audiences

For audiences who might not have immediate online access or for situations where you want to collect responses in person, using QR codes can be an effective strategy:

- Creating a QR Code: Microsoft Forms allows you to generate a QR code that links directly to your form. You can include this QR code on printed materials, such as flyers, posters, or business cards.

- Events and Conferences: Distribute the QR code at events, conferences, or workshops. Attendees can quickly scan the code with their smartphones to access the form.

- Stores and Physical Locations: Place QR codes in physical locations where your target audience is likely to be present, such as retail stores, restaurants, or community centers.

6. Integrating with Email Marketing Platforms

For organizations with a large contact list, integrating Microsoft Forms with email marketing platforms like MailChimp or Constant Contact can streamline the distribution process:

- Segmentation: Use your email marketing platform's segmentation tools to target specific groups within your audience. Tailor your messaging to these segments for better engagement.

- Automated Campaigns: Set up automated email campaigns that send the form to new subscribers or as part of a newsletter. This ensures consistent distribution over time.

- A/B Testing: Experiment with different email subject lines, body content, and call-to-action wording to see which variations yield the highest response rates.

7. Utilizing Internal Newsletters and Bulletins

For internal surveys, such as those targeting employees or members of an organization, internal newsletters or bulletins can be an effective distribution method:

- Highlighting the Survey: Feature the survey prominently in the newsletter, with a brief explanation of its purpose and a link to the form.

- Consistent Reminders: If the newsletter is recurring, include the survey in multiple editions to remind readers who may have missed it the first time.

- Departmental Distribution: For larger organizations, consider customizing the newsletter content for different departments or teams, focusing on how the survey relates to their specific roles.

8. Partnerships and Cross-Promotions

Collaborating with partners or other organizations can help you reach a broader audience:

- Joint Surveys: If your survey aligns with the interests of another organization, consider partnering to distribute the form. This can double your reach and provide more comprehensive data.

- Cross-Promotional Opportunities: Offer to distribute their surveys in exchange for them distributing yours. This mutual promotion can be beneficial for both parties.

9. Embedding in Mobile Apps

If your organization has a mobile app, embedding the form within the app can drive responses, especially if your audience frequently engages with the app:

- In-App Notifications: Use push notifications to alert users to the survey's availability. Ensure that the notification leads directly to the form for easy access.

- User Engagement Features: Incorporate the survey into a section of the app that users regularly visit, such as a dashboard or a user profile section.

10. Direct Messaging

Direct messaging platforms, such as WhatsApp, Slack, or even SMS, can be used to distribute your form for quick responses:

- Personalized Messages: Send personalized messages with the form link. Keep the message concise and emphasize the ease of filling out the form.

- Group Chats: Share the form in group chats where your target audience is active. For instance, if you're surveying a class, post the link in the class group chat.

- SMS Campaigns: For audiences with limited internet access or who prefer text messaging, send the form link via SMS. This is particularly effective for quick surveys.

11. Utilizing Video Content

Incorporating the form link within video content can engage visual learners and drive responses:

- Video Tutorials: If your form is related to training or feedback on a video, embed the form link directly within the video description or as an on-screen prompt.

- YouTube and Webinars: Share the form link during webinars or YouTube videos, particularly in the chat or comments section. Encourage viewers to complete the form after watching.

12. Gamification

Adding a gamified element to your form distribution can increase engagement and response rates:

- Quizzes with Rewards: Offer a small incentive or reward for completing a quiz. This could be a discount code, entry into a raffle, or points in a loyalty program.

- Leaderboard Challenges: Create a leaderboard for quiz participants to encourage competition, especially in an educational or corporate setting.

13. Offline Events and Flyers

If you're targeting a specific local community or hosting an event, consider using printed flyers with a QR code or link to the form:

- Event Handouts: Distribute handouts at events with the form link prominently displayed. Encourage attendees to fill out the form on-site or later.

- Community Boards: Post flyers in community centers, libraries, or other public spaces where your target audience frequents.

14. Personalized Outreach

Sometimes, a more personal approach is necessary to ensure high response rates:

- One-on-One Invitations: Reach out to key individuals or influencers within your audience who can encourage others to participate.

- Phone Calls: For critical surveys, a follow-up phone call to remind recipients to complete the form can be effective. This is particularly useful in B2B settings.

15. Ensuring Multi-Channel Distribution

Finally, combining several of the above strategies into a multi-channel approach ensures that you reach your audience in multiple ways, increasing the likelihood of responses:

Consistent Messaging: Ensure that your messaging is consistent across all channels. This reinforces the importance of the survey and can prompt those who may have ignored the first invitation to respond.

- Tracking and Adjusting: Use analytics to track which channels are most effective and adjust your distribution strategy accordingly. This can involve reallocating resources to more successful channels or modifying less effective ones.

By employing these effective distribution strategies, you can maximize the reach and response rate of your Microsoft Forms surveys and quizzes. The key to success is to understand your audience, leverage multiple channels, and make participation as simple and engaging as possible.

7.2.2 Incentivizing Participation

Incentivizing participation is a proven strategy to increase response rates for surveys and quizzes. By offering rewards or benefits, you create a compelling reason for participants to take the time and effort to complete your form. However, designing an effective incentive program requires careful planning and consideration to ensure that the incentives are both appealing to participants and cost-effective for your organization.

Understanding the Value of Incentives

Before diving into specific types of incentives, it's important to understand why incentives work. Participants often weigh the effort required to complete a survey or quiz against the potential benefits. If the perceived benefit outweighs the effort, they are more likely to participate. Incentives tip the balance in favor of participation by offering tangible rewards, thereby increasing the perceived value of taking part in your survey or quiz.

Types of Incentives

Incentives can take many forms, ranging from monetary rewards to non-monetary benefits. The key is to choose an incentive that aligns with your target audience's interests and motivations.

1. Monetary Incentives

Monetary incentives are one of the most effective ways to increase response rates. These can include cash prizes, gift cards, or discounts on products or services. The amount should be substantial enough to motivate participants but still within your budget. For example:

- Gift Cards: Offering a gift card to a popular retailer is a common and effective incentive. The amount could vary depending on the length and complexity of the survey or quiz.

- Cash Prizes: Conducting a draw for a cash prize among all participants is another effective strategy. This creates a sense of excitement and competition, encouraging more people to participate.

- Discounts or Coupons: Providing discounts on future purchases or services is particularly effective for businesses looking to drive customer engagement. This not only encourages survey completion but also promotes customer loyalty.

2. Non-Monetary Incentives

Non-monetary incentives can be just as effective as monetary ones, especially when they are aligned with the interests of your audience. Examples include:

- Exclusive Content: Offering access to exclusive content, such as a whitepaper, e-book, or webinar, can be a powerful motivator, particularly for professionals or individuals interested in a specific topic.

- Recognition and Social Incentives: For communities or teams, recognizing participants' contributions publicly can be a strong incentive. This could include featuring top contributors in a newsletter or giving shout-outs on social media.

- Charitable Donations: Offering to make a donation to a charity on behalf of the participant can appeal to those motivated by social causes. This not only encourages participation but also enhances your brand's image.

Designing an Effective Incentive Program

To design an effective incentive program, consider the following steps:

1. Identify Your Audience

Understanding your audience is crucial. Different groups are motivated by different incentives. For example, professionals may value access to exclusive content or networking opportunities, while students might prefer gift cards or discounts. Tailoring your incentive to your audience ensures that it is perceived as valuable.

2. Align Incentives with Your Goals

The incentive should align with the goals of your survey or quiz. For instance, if the goal is to gather customer feedback on a new product, offering a discount on that product might be more effective than a generic gift card. This not only encourages participation but also drives subsequent engagement with your product or service.

3. Set Clear Terms and Conditions

It's important to clearly communicate the terms and conditions of the incentive program. Participants should understand how and when they will receive their incentives, any eligibility requirements, and any deadlines for participation. Transparency builds trust and reduces the likelihood of disputes or dissatisfaction.

4. Promote the Incentive

Simply offering an incentive isn't enough; you need to promote it effectively. Highlight the incentive in your survey invitation, on social media, and on your website. Make sure potential participants understand the benefits of completing your survey or quiz.

5. Monitor and Evaluate

After the survey or quiz is complete, evaluate the effectiveness of your incentive program. Did the incentive lead to a significant increase in response rates? Was the cost of the incentive justified by the quality and quantity of the data collected? Use this information to refine your incentive strategy for future surveys or quizzes.

Ethical Considerations

While incentives can significantly boost response rates, it's important to consider the ethical implications. Overly aggressive incentivization can lead to biased responses, as participants may rush through the survey or quiz without providing thoughtful answers just to claim their reward. To mitigate this risk, ensure that the incentive is proportional to the effort required and that the survey or quiz design promotes genuine engagement.

Case Studies: Incentivizing Participation Successfully

Examining successful case studies can provide valuable insights into how to effectively implement incentives.

Case Study 1: A Retail Company's Survey Incentive Program

A well-known retail company wanted to gather customer feedback on a new line of products. To incentivize participation, they offered a $10 discount on future purchases to anyone who completed the survey. The result was a 40% increase in response rates compared to previous surveys without incentives. Additionally, the company noticed an uptick in sales, as customers returned to use their discounts.

Case Study 2: A Non-Profit Organization's Charitable Incentive

A non-profit organization conducted a survey to gather insights on public opinion regarding environmental issues. Instead of offering direct incentives to participants, they pledged to plant a tree for every completed survey. This approach resonated with their environmentally-conscious audience, leading to a 35% response rate, significantly higher than previous campaigns.

Case Study 3: An Educational Institution's Content-Driven Incentive

A university wanted to gather feedback from students on their online learning experience. They offered access to an exclusive webinar featuring a well-known industry expert as an incentive. The response rate was impressive, with 50% of the students participating, and the quality of the feedback was notably higher than previous surveys.

Best Practices for Incentivizing Participation

To maximize the effectiveness of your incentive program, consider the following best practices:

1. Tailor Incentives to Your Audience

Customize your incentives based on the demographics, interests, and preferences of your target audience. This personalization increases the perceived value of the incentive.

2. Keep It Simple

Make it easy for participants to understand how they can earn the incentive. Complex rules or conditions can deter participation. Ensure that the process is straightforward and transparent.

3. Test and Optimize

Before launching a large-scale incentive program, consider running a pilot test. This allows you to gauge the effectiveness of the incentive and make any necessary adjustments. Continually monitor response rates and feedback to optimize your approach over time.

4. Communicate Clearly

Ensure that the incentive is prominently featured in all communications related to the survey or quiz. Use clear, concise language to explain what the incentive is, how participants can earn it, and when they can expect to receive it.

5. Avoid Over-Incentivization

While incentives are powerful tools, they should not be the sole reason participants complete your survey or quiz. The content of the survey or quiz should be engaging and relevant to ensure that responses are thoughtful and meaningful.

Conclusion

Incentivizing participation is a strategic approach that can significantly enhance the response rates of your surveys and quizzes. By carefully selecting the right type of incentive, aligning it with your audience's interests, and implementing it ethically, you can gather higher-quality data that leads to actionable insights. Remember that the goal of incentivization is not just to increase quantity but also to maintain or improve the quality of the responses. When done correctly, incentives can be a win-win for both the organization and the participants, driving engagement and providing valuable feedback for decision-making.

7.3 Ensuring Data Privacy and Compliance

In today's digital age, data privacy is a critical concern for organizations and individuals alike. Microsoft Forms, as a tool for collecting information, must be used in a way that respects and protects the privacy of respondents. This section will guide you through the essentials of understanding and implementing privacy settings in Microsoft Forms, ensuring that your forms are compliant with relevant data protection regulations.

7.3.1 Understanding Privacy Settings

Data privacy is a multifaceted concept, encompassing how data is collected, stored, accessed, and shared. When using Microsoft Forms, it's essential to understand the built-in privacy features and how they can be configured to protect your respondents' data.

1. Importance of Data Privacy

Before diving into the specifics of privacy settings, it's important to understand why data privacy is crucial. Data privacy is not just about protecting information; it's about building trust with your respondents. When respondents trust that their data will be handled with care, they are more likely to participate and provide honest answers. Moreover, data privacy compliance is often a legal requirement, with severe penalties for breaches in many jurisdictions.

2. Microsoft Forms Privacy Overview

Microsoft Forms is part of the Microsoft 365 suite, which is designed with enterprise-grade security and privacy features. These features include data encryption, both in transit and at rest, and compliance with major international standards such as ISO/IEC 27001, GDPR, and HIPAA. However, understanding how to leverage these features effectively requires a closer look at the specific privacy settings available in Microsoft Forms.

3. Setting Up Privacy in Microsoft Forms

When you create a form, there are several settings you can adjust to control who can access the form, how the data is handled, and who can view the responses.

3.1. Control Who Can Respond

One of the first privacy settings to consider is controlling who can respond to your form. Microsoft Forms offers two primary options:

- Anyone with the link can respond: This setting makes your form public, allowing anyone who has the link to access and fill out the form. While this setting is convenient for surveys intended for a broad audience, it also means you have less control over who is submitting responses. Use this option when gathering data from a general audience where anonymity is acceptable or required.

- Only people in my organization can respond: This setting restricts access to individuals within your organization who have a Microsoft 365 account. This option is more secure and is ideal for internal surveys where you need to ensure that only authorized personnel provide input. It also allows you to track responses more accurately since responses can be linked to specific users.

For added security, you can further refine access by requiring that respondents sign in before submitting a response. This ensures that each submission is tied to a verifiable identity within your organization, reducing the risk of fraudulent or duplicate entries.

3.2. Anonymity and Response Tracking

Another key aspect of privacy in Microsoft Forms is deciding whether to collect responses anonymously or to track respondent identities.

- Anonymous Responses: In some cases, it's important to allow respondents to submit answers without revealing their identity. Anonymous responses encourage candid feedback, especially in sensitive surveys or quizzes where respondents might feel uncomfortable providing their name. To ensure anonymity, you can disable the option to record the respondent's name and email address. Remember that even when collecting anonymous responses, you must still handle the data responsibly and ensure that it cannot be traced back to individuals.

- Tracking Responses: In scenarios where it's important to know who is providing feedback—such as employee evaluations, compliance quizzes, or customer feedback forms—you can enable response tracking. This feature automatically records the respondent's name, email, and possibly other identifying information, depending on your organization's setup. This can be crucial for follow-up actions or for validating the authenticity of the data collected.

3.3. Data Storage and Access Control

Understanding where your data is stored and who has access to it is fundamental to maintaining privacy. Microsoft Forms stores data within the Microsoft 365 cloud infrastructure, which is subject to the same security measures that protect other Microsoft 365 services.

- Data Location: By default, data from Microsoft Forms is stored in the data center associated with your Microsoft 365 account's region. It's important to be aware of this, especially if your organization operates in multiple countries with different data residency requirements. You may need to consult your IT department or Microsoft support to ensure that your data is stored in a location that complies with local laws.

- Access Permissions: Only the form owner and those explicitly granted permissions can view the form responses. In Microsoft Forms, you can share response data with others by granting them view-only access or by sharing the entire form with co-owners who can manage it alongside you. Always review and adjust these permissions carefully to ensure that only authorized individuals can access sensitive data.

4. Handling Sensitive Data

When dealing with sensitive data, additional precautions are necessary. Sensitive data can include anything from personal identification numbers (PINs), financial information, health data, or any other data that could potentially harm the respondent if disclosed.

- Avoid Collecting Unnecessary Data: The best way to protect sensitive data is to avoid collecting it unless absolutely necessary. Before adding any question to your form, consider whether the information is essential for your purpose.

- Use Encryption: While Microsoft Forms automatically encrypts data in transit and at rest, if you are collecting particularly sensitive information, you might want to ensure additional encryption measures are in place, especially during the transmission of the data. Consult with your IT team to explore enhanced encryption options if necessary.

- Implement Data Masking: For certain types of sensitive information, consider using data masking techniques. This can include obscuring part of the data, such as showing only the last four digits of a credit card number, or using pseudonyms in place of actual names.

5. Complying with Data Retention Policies

Every organization should have a data retention policy that outlines how long data is kept and when it should be deleted. Microsoft Forms allows you to manage the lifecycle of your form data in accordance with these policies.

- Automatic Deletion of Data: Depending on your organization's compliance needs, you can set up policies that automatically delete form responses after a certain period. This reduces the risk of retaining outdated or unnecessary data, which could pose a privacy risk.

- Archiving Data: If you need to retain data for auditing purposes but do not need to keep it active, consider archiving the responses. Archived data can be stored in a secure location with restricted access, ensuring it is only available to those who need it.

- Disposing of Data: When the data is no longer needed, ensure it is permanently deleted from all systems, including any backups. Microsoft 365 provides tools to help with secure data deletion, ensuring that the data cannot be recovered once it has been erased.

6. Auditing and Monitoring Form Usage

Regularly auditing and monitoring how forms are used within your organization is a key aspect of maintaining privacy and compliance.

- Activity Logs: Microsoft 365 includes activity logging features that allow you to monitor how forms are being accessed and used. This includes who is creating, viewing, and modifying forms, as well as who is accessing the response data. Regular reviews of these logs can help you detect any unauthorized access or suspicious activity.

- Regular Audits: Conduct periodic audits of your forms and the data they collect. Ensure that all forms in use are still necessary and that they comply with your organization's data privacy policies. If you find any forms that no longer serve a purpose or that collect unnecessary data, consider deactivating or deleting them.

- Responding to Breaches: Despite best efforts, data breaches can still occur. It's crucial to have a response plan in place to address any breaches quickly. This should include notifying affected individuals, reporting the breach to relevant authorities, and taking steps to prevent future incidents.

7. Transparency and Communication with Respondents

Transparency with respondents about how their data will be used is not just a best practice; it is often a legal requirement.

- Providing a Privacy Statement: Include a clear and concise privacy statement at the beginning of your form. This statement should explain what data is being collected, how it will be used, who will have access to it, and how long it will be retained. Transparency builds trust and ensures that respondents are making an informed decision when they choose to provide their information.

- Obtaining Consent: In some cases, especially when collecting sensitive data or data for marketing purposes, you may need to obtain explicit consent from respondents. Microsoft Forms allows you to add a required consent checkbox that respondents must check before submitting the form. This ensures that they have acknowledged and agreed to your privacy policy.

- Allowing Respondents to Withdraw Consent: Provide respondents with a clear method to withdraw their consent and have their data removed from your records if they change their mind. This could be through a link to a form or a contact email provided in the privacy statement.

8. Compliance with Global and Local Regulations

Finally, it's important to ensure that your use of Microsoft Forms complies with relevant global and local data protection regulations.

- General Data Protection Regulation (GDPR): If you are operating in the European Union or collecting data from EU citizens, GDPR compliance is mandatory. GDPR requires that you obtain explicit consent for data collection, provide the right to access and delete data, and ensure that data is processed securely.

- California Consumer Privacy Act (CCPA): For organizations operating in California, or collecting data from California residents, CCPA imposes similar requirements to GDPR, including providing the right to opt-out of data collection and the right to delete personal data.

- Health Insurance Portability and Accountability Act (HIPAA): If your forms are collecting health-related information in the United States, you must comply with HIPAA. This includes ensuring that any collected data is stored and transmitted securely and that only authorized personnel can access it.

- Local Regulations: In addition to these major regulations, be aware of any local data protection laws that may apply to your organization. This could include laws specific to your industry or region that impose additional requirements on data handling.

By understanding and properly configuring the privacy settings in Microsoft Forms, you can ensure that your forms and quizzes not only meet your data collection needs but also respect the privacy of your respondents and comply with legal requirements. This approach will help you build trust with your audience, minimize the risk of data breaches, and maintain compliance with data protection regulations.

7.3.2 GDPR and Other Regulations

1. Understanding GDPR and Its Impact on Data Collection

The General Data Protection Regulation (GDPR) is a comprehensive data protection law enacted by the European Union (EU) that came into effect on May 25, 2018. GDPR aims to protect the privacy and personal data of individuals within the EU and EEA (European Economic Area). It imposes strict rules on how organizations collect, store, and process personal data.

If you are using Microsoft Forms to collect data from EU citizens or residents, GDPR compliance is mandatory, regardless of where your organization is based. Failure to comply with GDPR can result in hefty fines and damage to your reputation.

Key Principles of GDPR:

- Lawfulness, Fairness, and Transparency: Data must be processed lawfully, fairly, and in a transparent manner. This means you need to have a clear and lawful basis for data collection, and respondents should be fully informed about how their data will be used.

- Purpose Limitation: Data should only be collected for specific, explicit, and legitimate purposes. It must not be further processed in a manner that is incompatible with those purposes.

- Data Minimization: Only data that is necessary for the intended purpose should be collected. Avoid collecting excessive information that is not directly relevant to your survey or quiz.

- Accuracy: Personal data must be accurate and kept up to date. Any inaccurate data should be corrected or deleted without delay.

- Storage Limitation: Data should not be kept longer than necessary. You must establish retention periods and ensure data is deleted or anonymized when it is no longer needed.

- Integrity and Confidentiality: Data must be processed in a way that ensures its security, including protection against unauthorized or unlawful processing and against accidental loss, destruction, or damage.

- Accountability: As a data controller, you are responsible for and must be able to demonstrate compliance with GDPR.

2. Implementing GDPR Compliance in Microsoft Forms

To ensure GDPR compliance when using Microsoft Forms, consider the following steps:

A. Informing Respondents:

- Privacy Notice: Include a clear privacy notice at the beginning of your form. This notice should inform respondents about the purpose of the data collection, how their data will be used, who will have access to it, and how long it will be retained. Additionally, it should provide contact information for any data protection inquiries.

- Consent: Explicit consent is required for data processing under GDPR. Include a consent checkbox in your form where respondents can agree to the processing of their personal data. Ensure that this checkbox is not pre-checked, and respondents can only proceed after giving their consent.

B. Data Minimization and Purpose Limitation:

- Relevance of Questions: Review the questions in your survey or quiz to ensure they are directly relevant to the stated purpose. Avoid asking for unnecessary personal information, such as age, gender, or location, unless it is essential for your analysis.

- Anonymization: Whenever possible, anonymize responses to protect the identities of respondents. Anonymization involves removing or encrypting personal identifiers, making it impossible to trace the data back to an individual.

C. Secure Data Handling:

- Data Encryption: Microsoft Forms uses encryption to protect data during transmission and storage. Ensure that your organization's overall data handling procedures also involve encryption, especially if data is exported from Microsoft Forms to other systems.

- Access Control: Limit access to the collected data to only those who need it for analysis or reporting purposes. Use Microsoft 365's role-based access controls to manage who can view, edit, or delete responses.

D. Respondent Rights:

Under GDPR, respondents have several rights regarding their data, including the right to access, rectify, or erase their data, and the right to object to its processing. You must have procedures in place to respond to such requests in a timely manner.

- Right to Access: Respondents can request access to their data. Ensure you can provide them with a copy of their responses in a structured, commonly used, and machine-readable format.

- Right to Rectification: If a respondent identifies any errors in their data, you must correct it promptly. Microsoft Forms allows you to manually update responses if necessary.

- Right to Erasure: Respondents can request the deletion of their data. Ensure that you have a process in place to delete individual responses both in Microsoft Forms and any other systems where the data has been exported.

E. Data Retention and Deletion:

- Retention Policy: Define a data retention policy that specifies how long you will keep the collected data. This period should align with the purpose of the data collection. Once the retention period expires, the data should be securely deleted or anonymized.

- Automatic Deletion: If you regularly collect data using Microsoft Forms, consider setting up automatic deletion schedules to ensure compliance with your retention policy.

3. Complying with Other Regulations

In addition to GDPR, other regions and industries have their own data protection regulations. It is important to be aware of these regulations and ensure compliance when using Microsoft Forms.

A. California Consumer Privacy Act (CCPA):

The California Consumer Privacy Act (CCPA) is a state law that enhances privacy rights and consumer protection for residents of California, USA. CCPA gives consumers the right to know what personal data is being collected about them, to whom it is being sold, and the right to access and delete their data.

- Similarities with GDPR: Like GDPR, CCPA requires businesses to be transparent about data collection and allows consumers to access and delete their personal information.

- Key Differences: Unlike GDPR, CCPA applies to for-profit entities that meet certain thresholds, such as having annual revenues over $25 million. CCPA also requires businesses to provide an opt-out mechanism for data selling.

B. Health Insurance Portability and Accountability Act (HIPAA):

HIPAA is a US law that sets national standards for the protection of health information. If you are collecting health-related data using Microsoft Forms, ensure that your forms comply with HIPAA requirements.

- Protected Health Information (PHI): If your form collects PHI, such as medical history, health conditions, or treatment information, you must implement strict security measures, including encryption and access controls.

- HIPAA Compliance in Microsoft Forms: While Microsoft 365 offers HIPAA compliance features, ensure that your organization's use of Microsoft Forms aligns with HIPAA's security and privacy rules.

C. Family Educational Rights and Privacy Act (FERPA):

FERPA is a US federal law that protects the privacy of student education records. If you are using Microsoft Forms in an educational setting to collect student data, FERPA compliance is essential.

- Student Data: Ensure that student information collected through Microsoft Forms is protected and only accessible to authorized personnel. Parents and eligible students have the right to access and request corrections to their education records.

D. Personal Data Protection Act (PDPA):

The Personal Data Protection Act (PDPA) is a data protection law in Singapore that governs the collection, use, and disclosure of personal data by organizations. PDPA is similar to GDPR but tailored to the Singaporean context.

- Consent Requirements: PDPA requires organizations to obtain consent before collecting personal data. Ensure that your Microsoft Forms include a clear consent mechanism.

- Data Breach Notification: Under PDPA, organizations must notify the relevant authorities and affected individuals in the event of a data breach. Implement procedures to detect and respond to data breaches promptly.

4. Best Practices for Data Privacy and Compliance

To ensure compliance with GDPR and other data protection regulations, follow these best practices when using Microsoft Forms:

A. Conduct a Data Protection Impact Assessment (DPIA):

Before launching a new survey or quiz that collects personal data, conduct a DPIA to assess the potential risks to data privacy. This assessment will help you identify and mitigate any privacy risks associated with your form.

B. Regularly Review and Update Privacy Policies:

Ensure that your organization's privacy policies are up-to-date and reflect the latest legal requirements. Regularly review your policies and update them as necessary to ensure ongoing compliance.

C. Train Staff on Data Privacy:

Provide training to staff who use Microsoft Forms on the importance of data privacy and compliance. Ensure they are aware of the procedures for handling data securely and responding to data subject requests.

D. Monitor Data Processing Activities:

Keep track of how data collected through Microsoft Forms is processed and stored. Regularly audit your data processing activities to ensure compliance with your organization's data protection policies.

E. Engage Legal and Compliance Experts:

Consult with legal and compliance experts to ensure that your use of Microsoft Forms aligns with relevant data protection laws. This is especially important if you are operating in multiple jurisdictions with different regulations.

Conclusion:

Ensuring data privacy and compliance when using Microsoft Forms is not only a legal obligation but also a key factor in building trust with your respondents. By following the guidelines outlined in this section, you can confidently use Microsoft Forms to collect data while respecting the privacy rights of your respondents and complying with regulations such as GDPR, CCPA, HIPAA, and others.

CHAPTER VIII
Troubleshooting and Support

8.1 Common Issues and Solutions

8.1.1 Form Submission Problems

Form submission problems can hinder the effectiveness of your surveys and quizzes in Microsoft Forms. This section addresses common issues and provides detailed solutions to ensure a smooth user experience.

1. Troubleshooting Form Submission Issues

1.1 Error Messages During Submission

Users may encounter various error messages when attempting to submit a form. These errors can range from connectivity issues to form configuration problems. Common error messages include:

- "Form submission failed": This message may appear if there is a network issue or if the form has not been configured correctly.

- "You cannot submit this form": This could indicate that the form has been closed or that the user is not authorized to submit responses.

- "Required fields missing": This message appears if the user has not filled out all mandatory fields in the form.

Solutions:

- Check Form Settings: Ensure that the form is open for submissions. Verify that the form settings allow responses and that the submission deadline has not passed.

- Verify Internet Connection: Users should check their internet connection to ensure it's stable. If necessary, they should refresh the page or try a different network.

- Review Required Fields: Ensure that all required fields are correctly marked and that users are filling them out. Adjust the form settings if needed to provide clear instructions on mandatory fields.

1.2 Browser Compatibility Issues

Form submissions may fail if users are using outdated or incompatible web browsers. Microsoft Forms supports modern browsers such as Microsoft Edge, Google Chrome, and Mozilla Firefox. Issues can arise if users are using older versions or less common browsers.

Solutions:

- Update Browsers: Advise users to update their browsers to the latest version. Modern browsers are more likely to be compatible with Microsoft Forms.

- Switch Browsers: If updating does not resolve the issue, users should try accessing the form using a different browser that is known to be compatible with Microsoft Forms.

- Clear Cache and Cookies: Sometimes, clearing the browser's cache and cookies can resolve submission problems. Users can do this through their browser settings.

1.3 Form Limits and Restrictions

Microsoft Forms has certain limits and restrictions that can impact form submissions. These include limits on the number of responses, file size, and the number of questions per form.

Solutions:

- Check Response Limits: Verify if the form has reached its response limit. If the form is intended to collect more responses, consider upgrading the Microsoft 365 plan or creating a new form.

- Review File Size Limits: Ensure that any file uploads adhere to Microsoft Forms' file size restrictions. Users may need to reduce the file size or format before submission.

- Simplify the Form: If the form is too complex or lengthy, consider breaking it into multiple forms or simplifying the questions to make it more user-friendly.

2. Resolving Data Export Issues

2.1 Problems with Exporting Data to Excel

Users may encounter issues when exporting form responses to Excel. Common problems include:

- "Export failed": This error may occur if there is a problem with the form data or if the connection to Excel is interrupted.

- "Data is not displaying correctly": Sometimes, the exported data may not appear as expected due to formatting issues or errors during export.

Solutions:

- Check Data Integrity: Ensure that the form data is complete and that there are no errors or inconsistencies that could affect the export process.

- Export in Smaller Batches: If the form has a large amount of data, try exporting in smaller batches to avoid performance issues.

- Update Excel: Ensure that Excel is up-to-date and compatible with the data format being exported. Sometimes, updating Excel can resolve compatibility issues.

2.2 Issues with Formulas and Calculations

When exporting data, formulas or calculations may not work correctly in Excel if the data is not formatted properly or if there are discrepancies between the data types.

Solutions:

- Review Formulas: Check the formulas used in Excel to ensure they are correctly applied to the exported data. Adjust the formulas as needed to match the data format.

- Format Data Correctly: Ensure that the data is formatted correctly in Excel to avoid issues with calculations. Use Excel's formatting tools to adjust data types and formats as necessary.

3. Handling Response and Data Management Issues

3.1 Inaccurate or Incomplete Responses

Sometimes, form responses may be inaccurate or incomplete due to user error or system glitches.

Solutions:

- Review Response Settings: Check the form settings to ensure that validation rules are properly configured to minimize incomplete or inaccurate responses.

- Provide Clear Instructions: Ensure that the form provides clear instructions and examples to help users complete it accurately.

- Follow Up with Respondents: If possible, follow up with respondents to clarify any inaccuracies or request additional information.

3.2 Data Integrity Issues

Maintaining data integrity is crucial for accurate analysis. Problems can arise from data corruption or discrepancies during collection.

Solutions:

- Regularly Backup Data: Regularly back up form data to prevent loss or corruption. This can be done by exporting data periodically.

- Monitor for Anomalies: Watch for any anomalies or unusual patterns in the data. Investigate and address any issues promptly to maintain data quality.

4. Best Practices for Avoiding Submission Problems

4.1 Testing Forms Before Launch

Thoroughly test forms before distributing them to ensure they work as expected.

Solutions:

- Conduct Internal Testing: Test the form with a small group of users to identify and resolve any issues before wider distribution.

- Use Test Responses: Submit test responses to check for any issues with submission and data collection.

4.2 Providing User Support

Offer support to users who may encounter issues with form submissions.

Solutions:

- Create Help Resources: Provide users with help resources, such as FAQs or troubleshooting guides, to assist with common issues.

- Offer Contact Support: Provide contact information for support if users need additional assistance with form submissions.

4.3 Keeping Forms Updated

Regularly update forms to address any issues and improve functionality.

Solutions:

- Review and Revise Forms: Periodically review and revise forms to ensure they meet current needs and address any issues identified during use.

- Implement Feedback: Gather feedback from users to identify areas for improvement and make necessary updates to the form.

By addressing these common form submission problems and implementing the solutions provided, you can enhance the effectiveness of your Microsoft Forms and ensure a smooth experience for both you and your respondents.

8.1.2 Data Export Issues

Data export issues can be frustrating, especially when dealing with large volumes of information collected via Microsoft Forms. These issues often stem from a variety of sources, including technical glitches, incorrect settings, or data compatibility problems. In this section, we will explore common data export issues and provide detailed solutions to address them effectively.

1. Understanding Data Export in Microsoft Forms

Before diving into troubleshooting, it is essential to understand how data export works in Microsoft Forms:

- Export Formats: Microsoft Forms allows you to export response data primarily in Excel format. This format is widely used and facilitates further data manipulation and analysis.

- Export Process: To export data from Microsoft Forms, navigate to the Responses tab of your form and click on the "Open in Excel" button. This action downloads an Excel file containing all the responses.

2. Common Data Export Issues

2.1. Missing Data in Exported Files

One of the most common issues is missing data in the exported file. This can occur for various reasons:

- Incomplete Responses: If respondents have not completed the form fully, their incomplete data may not appear in the export.

- Filtering and Sorting Issues: Sometimes, data might be inadvertently filtered or sorted incorrectly in the Excel file.

- Technical Glitches: Occasionally, technical issues during the export process can lead to missing data.

Solution:

1. Verify Responses: Check the Microsoft Forms dashboard to ensure that all responses are recorded. Verify if the missing data is present in the online form interface.

2. Check for Incomplete Responses: Look for any responses that are marked as incomplete or partial. These entries may not appear in the export file.

3. Re-export the Data: Attempt to export the data again. Sometimes, re-exporting can resolve temporary glitches.

4. Use Data Analysis Tools: Utilize Excel's built-in tools like filtering, sorting, and conditional formatting to identify and address any inconsistencies in the data.

2.2. Export File Format Issues

Issues related to file format can also arise:

- File Compatibility: Occasionally, the exported Excel file may have compatibility issues with certain versions of Excel or other spreadsheet software.

- Corrupted Files: Files may become corrupted during download or if there are issues with the internet connection.

Solution:

1. Check File Compatibility: Ensure that you are using a version of Excel that is compatible with the file format. Microsoft Forms exports data in .xlsx format, which is supported by most recent versions of Excel.

2. Repair Corrupted Files: If the file appears corrupted, try to open it with another spreadsheet application like Google Sheets or LibreOffice. If successful, save it in a different format and try opening it again with Excel.

3. Download Again: Re-download the export file to see if the issue persists. Ensure that your internet connection is stable during the download process.

2.3. Data Formatting Issues

Formatting issues can affect how data appears in the exported file:

- Incorrect Data Types: Sometimes, data may not be formatted correctly, such as dates or numbers being displayed as text.

- Merged Cells or Layout Issues: Merged cells or unexpected layout changes can cause confusion in the exported file.

Solution:

1. Format Cells in Excel: Open the Excel file and adjust cell formats as needed. For example, set columns with dates to the correct date format or convert text to numbers where necessary.

2. Unmerge Cells: If merged cells are causing layout problems, unmerge them and adjust the layout to ensure that data is displayed correctly.

3. Review Data Layout: Check the layout of the data to ensure it matches the structure expected from Microsoft Forms. Adjust as needed for clarity and usability.

2.4. Large Data Volume Issues

Handling large volumes of data can present unique challenges:

- Performance Issues: Exporting large datasets may cause performance issues, such as long processing times or application crashes.

- File Size Limitations: Some spreadsheet applications have file size limitations that can affect the usability of large export files.

Solution:

1. Use Data Filtering: Before exporting, consider applying filters to reduce the volume of data being exported at once. Export smaller chunks if necessary.

2. Optimize Excel Performance: Ensure that Excel is optimized for handling large files by closing other applications and increasing available memory.

3. Split Data into Multiple Files: If the data volume is too large, export it in segments or split the file into multiple smaller files for easier handling.

2.5. Security and Privacy Concerns

Exporting sensitive or confidential data can raise security and privacy issues:

- Data Security: Ensuring that exported data is handled securely is crucial to prevent unauthorized access or breaches.

- Compliance Issues: Exported data must comply with relevant data protection regulations and organizational policies.

Solution:

1. Implement Data Security Measures: Store the exported file in a secure location with restricted access. Use encryption if needed to protect sensitive information.

2. Review Data Protection Policies: Ensure that the handling and storage of exported data comply with data protection regulations such as GDPR or CCPA.

3. Access Control: Limit access to the exported data to authorized personnel only and implement access controls as per organizational guidelines.

3. Troubleshooting Steps

When facing export issues, follow these troubleshooting steps to resolve them:

1. Identify the Issue: Determine the specific nature of the problem, whether it's missing data, formatting issues, or performance-related.

2. Consult Microsoft Support: If the issue persists, consult Microsoft's support resources for guidance. They may offer specific solutions or updates.

3. Check Community Forums: Explore Microsoft community forums and user groups for similar issues and solutions shared by other users.

4. Update Software: Ensure that Microsoft Forms and Excel are updated to the latest versions, as updates may fix known issues or improve functionality.

5. Test in Different Environments: Try exporting the data on a different computer or network to rule out environmental factors.

By following these detailed solutions and troubleshooting steps, you can effectively address common data export issues in Microsoft Forms and ensure a smooth and efficient data handling process.

8.2 Accessing Microsoft Support

8.2.1 Using Microsoft Help Resources

Introduction to Microsoft Help Resources

Microsoft provides a range of help resources designed to support users in navigating and troubleshooting issues with Microsoft Forms. These resources are invaluable for both novice and experienced users seeking solutions to problems or wishing to learn more about the application's features. Utilizing these resources can enhance your efficiency and ensure that you are making the most out of Microsoft Forms.

1. Microsoft Forms Help Center

1.1 Overview

The Microsoft Forms Help Center is the primary resource for finding answers to common questions and issues related to Microsoft Forms. It provides a comprehensive collection of articles, how-to guides, and troubleshooting tips.

1.2 Accessing the Help Center

To access the Microsoft Forms Help Center, follow these steps:

1. Open Microsoft Forms.

2. Click on the "Help" icon (typically represented by a question mark) located in the upper right corner of the Forms interface.

3. Select "Help & Learning" from the dropdown menu. This will redirect you to the Microsoft Forms Help Center on the web.

1.3 Navigating the Help Center

The Help Center is organized into several sections:

- Getting Started: This section provides introductory guides on using Microsoft Forms, including how to create forms, customize them, and analyze responses.

- Features and Functions: Detailed articles on specific features, such as question types, form settings, and data export options.

- Troubleshooting: Common issues and their solutions, including error messages and technical problems.

- FAQs: Frequently asked questions covering a range of topics from basic to advanced.

1.4 Using Search and Filters

The Help Center includes a search bar at the top of the page. Enter keywords related to your issue or query to quickly find relevant articles. Filters can also help narrow down search results by category or topic.

2. Microsoft Support Documentation

2.1 Overview

Microsoft Support Documentation provides detailed, technical explanations and instructions on using Microsoft Forms and other Microsoft 365 applications. It is a valuable resource for users seeking in-depth knowledge and advanced troubleshooting guidance.

2.2 Accessing Documentation

To access the Microsoft Support Documentation:

1. Visit the [Microsoft Support website](https://support.microsoft.com).

2. Use the search bar to enter "Microsoft Forms" and explore the available documents.

2.3 Types of Documentation

The documentation includes:

- User Guides: Detailed guides covering the full spectrum of Microsoft Forms features and functionalities.

- Technical Articles: In-depth articles addressing technical aspects and advanced configurations.

- Release Notes: Information on the latest updates and new features added to Microsoft Forms.

2.4 Using Documentation Effectively

Documentation can be extensive. Use the search feature to find specific topics, and bookmark useful articles for future reference. Pay attention to version-specific notes to ensure that the guidance applies to your version of Microsoft Forms.

3. Microsoft Learn and Training

3.1 Overview

Microsoft Learn is an online platform offering free, interactive learning paths and modules. It includes training content tailored to Microsoft Forms and other Microsoft 365 applications.

3.2 Accessing Microsoft Learn

To access Microsoft Learn:

1. Go to [Microsoft Learn](https://learn.microsoft.com).

2. Use the search bar to find learning paths related to Microsoft Forms.

3.3 Learning Paths and Modules

Microsoft Learn provides structured learning paths and individual modules:

- Learning Paths: Comprehensive courses covering various aspects of Microsoft Forms, often including quizzes and hands-on labs.

- Modules: Focused tutorials on specific features or tasks, such as creating forms, customizing them, and analyzing data.

3.4 Using Training Resources

Complete learning paths for a thorough understanding, or select individual modules for targeted learning. Engage with interactive content to practice and apply what you've learned.

4. Microsoft Community Forums

4.1 Overview

The Microsoft Community Forums are user-driven discussion boards where you can ask questions, share experiences, and seek advice from other Microsoft Forms users and experts.

4.2 Accessing the Forums

To access the Microsoft Community Forums:

1. Visit the [Microsoft Community website](https://answers.microsoft.com).

2. Navigate to the Microsoft Forms category to view relevant discussions and threads.

4.3 Participating in the Community

- Asking Questions: Post your questions or issues to receive answers from the community.

- Answering Questions: Contribute by providing solutions or insights based on your own experiences.

- Searching Existing Threads: Many common issues are discussed in existing threads, so use the search function to find answers quickly.

4.4 Following Up

Monitor your posts for responses and engage in follow-up discussions to resolve issues effectively. Participate in discussions to stay updated with new solutions and best practices.

5. Microsoft Customer Support

5.1 Overview

For more personalized assistance, you can contact Microsoft Customer Support directly. This option is particularly useful for unresolved technical issues or specific account-related inquiries.

5.2 Contacting Support

To contact Microsoft Customer Support:

1. Visit the [Microsoft Support website](https://support.microsoft.com).

2. Click on "Contact Support" and select "Microsoft Forms" as the product you need help with.

3. Choose your preferred contact method, such as chat, phone support, or email.

5.3 What to Provide

When contacting support, provide:

- A detailed description of the issue: Include any error messages and steps you've already taken to troubleshoot.

- Screenshots or error codes: Attach relevant images or codes to help support diagnose the problem.

- Account information: Include your Microsoft account details if needed for verification.

5.4 Following Up

Keep track of your support request and follow up if necessary. Ensure that any issues are fully resolved before closing the support case.

Conclusion

Using Microsoft Help resources effectively can significantly enhance your experience with Microsoft Forms. By leveraging the Help Center, support documentation, learning paths, community forums, and direct customer support, you can efficiently troubleshoot issues, expand your knowledge, and resolve any challenges you encounter. Regularly utilizing these resources ensures that you stay informed about updates and best practices, making your use of Microsoft Forms more productive and effective.

8.2.2 Community Forums and User Groups

In the world of Microsoft Forms, community forums and user groups can be invaluable resources. They offer platforms for users to exchange ideas, seek advice, and troubleshoot issues with the support of a broader community. This section will guide you through the best practices for engaging with community forums and user groups, providing a detailed approach to maximizing the benefits of these resources.

Understanding the Value of Community Forums and User Groups

Community forums and user groups are online platforms where users of Microsoft Forms and other Microsoft 365 applications can interact. These platforms provide a space for users to ask questions, share experiences, and collaborate on solving common issues. The collective knowledge and experience found in these forums and groups can be incredibly beneficial for both new and experienced users.

1. Community Forums: These are online discussion boards where users can post questions, share solutions, and engage in discussions about various topics related to Microsoft Forms. Popular forums include the Microsoft Community Forums and tech-related sites like Reddit or Stack Exchange.

2. User Groups: These are more structured and often localized groups where users meet either virtually or in person. They can be specific to certain regions, industries, or areas of interest. User groups often have regular meetings, webinars, and events where members can network and learn from each other.

How to Effectively Use Community Forums

1. Choosing the Right Forum:

 - Microsoft Community Forums: This is the official forum hosted by Microsoft where users can find threads related to all Microsoft products, including Microsoft Forms. It's a reliable source of information and often monitored by Microsoft experts.

 - Reddit: Subreddits like r/MicrosoftForms and r/Office365 are active communities where users share tips and discuss issues.

 - Stack Exchange: The Microsoft Stack Exchange network offers a dedicated section for Office 365, which includes Microsoft Forms.

2. Creating a Useful Post:

 - Be Specific: When posting a question, include as many details as possible. Describe the problem you are facing, the steps you've already taken to troubleshoot, and any error messages or screenshots that might help others understand your issue.

 - Use Clear Titles: Create a descriptive and concise title for your post to attract users who are knowledgeable about the issue you're facing.

- Follow Up: After posting, monitor responses and engage with those who provide solutions or additional questions. Acknowledge helpful responses and provide feedback on what worked for you.

3. Participating in Discussions:

- Share Your Knowledge: If you have expertise or solutions to common problems, contribute by answering questions and providing guidance to others.

- Be Respectful: Maintain a polite and respectful tone in all interactions. Constructive discussions lead to better outcomes and foster a positive community environment.

4. Searching for Existing Solutions:

- Use Search Functions: Before posting a new question, use the search functionality to check if your issue has already been discussed. This can save time and provide immediate answers to common problems.

5. Utilizing Tags and Categories:

- Tag Appropriately: Use relevant tags and categories when posting to ensure that your question reaches users who specialize in that area. This helps in getting more accurate and helpful responses.

Engaging with User Groups

1. Finding User Groups:

- Microsoft User Groups: Search for official Microsoft user groups or events through the Microsoft Tech Community or Microsoft's local user groups.

- LinkedIn and Facebook: Many user groups operate on social media platforms. Look for groups focused on Microsoft Forms or Office 365.

- Meetup.com: This platform hosts information about local tech meetups and user groups, which can be great for networking and learning.

2. Participating in User Group Events:

- Attend Meetings: Join virtual or in-person meetings to interact with other users and experts. These meetings often feature presentations, discussions, and Q&A sessions.

- Network with Peers: Use these opportunities to connect with others who have similar interests or expertise. Networking can lead to valuable insights and collaborations.

3. Engaging in Webinars and Workshops:

- Register for Webinars: Many user groups and Microsoft itself offer webinars on various topics related to Microsoft Forms. Participating in these can provide in-depth knowledge and hands-on experience.

- Participate Actively: Engage in Q&A sessions during webinars and workshops to get your specific questions addressed.

4. Contributing to Group Discussions:

- Share Your Experiences: Contribute by discussing your experiences with Microsoft Forms, sharing tips, and offering advice based on your own usage.

- Provide Feedback: If you have suggestions for improvements or feedback on Microsoft Forms, share these with the group. Your input can contribute to better practices and future updates.

Benefits of Community Engagement

1. Access to Expert Knowledge:

- Diverse Expertise: Community forums and user groups offer access to a wide range of expertise and experiences. This can be especially useful for troubleshooting complex issues or learning advanced techniques.

2. Learning Opportunities:

- Best Practices: Engaging with the community allows you to learn best practices and new strategies for using Microsoft Forms more effectively.

- Updates and Trends: Stay informed about the latest updates, features, and trends related to Microsoft Forms by participating in discussions and attending events.

3. Networking and Collaboration:

- Building Connections: Networking with other users can lead to valuable connections and potential collaborations on projects or solutions.

- Peer Support: Being part of a community provides emotional and practical support from peers who understand the challenges and successes of using Microsoft Forms.

Conclusion

Community forums and user groups are essential resources for anyone looking to enhance their use of Microsoft Forms. By actively participating in these platforms, you can gain insights, solve problems, and connect with other users. Whether you are seeking solutions to specific issues or looking to share your knowledge, these resources provide a collaborative environment that can significantly enhance your experience with Microsoft Forms.

8.3 Keeping Your Forms Up-to-Date

Keeping your Microsoft Forms up-to-date is crucial for ensuring that the data you collect remains relevant, accurate, and useful. Regular updates to your forms can help maintain engagement, address any emerging issues, and improve the overall user experience. This section will guide you through the steps and best practices for updating your existing forms.

8.3.1 Updating Existing Forms

Updating existing forms involves several steps, including evaluating the current form's performance, making necessary changes, testing the updated form, and communicating these changes to your respondents. Here's a detailed guide on how to effectively update your forms:

Step 1: Evaluate the Current Form

Before making any updates, it's important to assess how the current form is performing. Consider the following aspects:

1. Response Rates: Check if the number of responses is as expected. A low response rate might indicate that the form is too long, confusing, or unengaging.

2. Data Quality: Evaluate the quality of the data you're receiving. Are the responses accurate and useful? Are there any patterns of incomplete or irrelevant answers?

3. User Feedback: Gather feedback from respondents if possible. This can be done through a follow-up survey or direct communication with some of the participants.

4. Technical Issues: Identify any technical problems that respondents might be facing, such as difficulties in submitting the form or accessing it on different devices.

Step 2: Plan Your Updates

Based on your evaluation, plan the changes that need to be made. This could include:

1. Question Modifications: Adjusting or rewriting questions for clarity and relevance. Remove any questions that are not providing useful data and add new ones if necessary.

2. Design and Layout Improvements: Make the form more user-friendly. This could involve simplifying the layout, improving the visual design, or making the form more accessible.

3. Technical Fixes: Address any technical issues that were identified. This might involve changing settings, fixing bugs, or ensuring compatibility across devices and browsers.

Step 3: Make the Updates

Once you've planned the necessary changes, you can start updating the form. Follow these steps:

1. Access the Form: Go to Microsoft Forms and open the form you want to update.

2. Edit Questions: Click on the question you want to edit. You can change the question type, wording, options, and any branching logic.

3. Add New Questions: Use the "Add New" button to insert new questions. Choose the appropriate question type (e.g., multiple choice, text, rating) based on your needs.

4. Reorder Questions: Drag and drop questions to change their order if necessary. This can help improve the flow of the form.

5. Design Changes: Click on the "Theme" button to change the form's theme. Customize colors, fonts, and background images to enhance the visual appeal.

6. Settings Adjustments: Go to the form settings (click on the ellipsis (...) in the top right corner) to adjust settings like who can respond, start and end dates, response receipts, and more.

Step 4: Test the Updated Form

Before distributing the updated form, it's crucial to test it thoroughly to ensure everything works as expected. Follow these steps:

1. Preview the Form: Use the "Preview" button to see how the form looks and functions on different devices (e.g., desktop, tablet, mobile).

2. Test All Features: Go through the entire form, answering all questions and testing any branching logic or conditional questions.

3. Submit a Test Response: Submit the form to check if the responses are being recorded correctly and if any confirmation messages or emails are sent as intended.

4. Ask for Feedback: If possible, ask a few colleagues or friends to test the form and provide feedback on any issues or areas for improvement.

Step 5: Communicate Changes to Respondents

If you have already distributed the form and received responses, it's important to communicate any significant changes to your respondents. Here's how you can do this:

1. Send an Email Update: Inform respondents about the changes via email. Explain why the updates were made and how they can access the updated form.

2. Update Instructions: If the form is embedded on a website or shared through a link, update any instructions or descriptions to reflect the changes.

3. Acknowledge Feedback: If the updates were made based on respondent feedback, acknowledge this in your communication. This can help build trust and encourage further participation.

Step 6: Monitor and Maintain

After updating the form and redistributing it, continue to monitor its performance and maintain it regularly. Consider these best practices:

1. Regular Reviews: Periodically review the form's performance and make further updates as needed. This ensures that the form remains relevant and effective over time.

2. Stay Updated: Keep up with any updates or new features in Microsoft Forms. Integrating new functionalities can improve your forms and the data collection process.

3. Backup Data: Regularly export and backup your form responses. This protects your data in case of any issues with the form or the platform.

4. Feedback Loop: Continue to collect and act on feedback from respondents. This ongoing process helps you refine your forms and improve the user experience.

Tips for Effective Form Updates

To ensure your updates are effective and enhance the user experience, consider the following tips:

1. Clarity and Simplicity: Keep questions clear and concise. Avoid jargon and complex language that might confuse respondents.

2. Consistency: Maintain a consistent format and style throughout the form. This helps respondents navigate the form more easily.

3. Accessibility: Ensure your form is accessible to all users, including those with disabilities. Use accessible design practices and test with assistive technologies.

4. Engagement: Use engaging elements like images, videos, and interactive questions to keep respondents interested and motivated to complete the form.

5. Feedback Mechanism: Include a way for respondents to provide feedback on the form itself. This can help you identify issues and areas for improvement more quickly.

By following these steps and best practices, you can keep your Microsoft Forms up-to-date, ensuring that they continue to meet your data collection needs and provide valuable insights. Regular updates not only enhance the user experience but also improve the quality and reliability of the data you collect.

8.3.2 Maintaining Data Integrity

Maintaining data integrity is a critical aspect of using Microsoft Forms effectively, particularly when the data collected is essential for decision-making, compliance, or reporting purposes. Data integrity refers to the accuracy, consistency, and reliability of data throughout its lifecycle. In the context of Microsoft Forms, this means ensuring that the data you collect through forms and quizzes remains accurate, unaltered, and accessible as needed.

Understanding Data Integrity in Microsoft Forms

Before diving into the specifics of maintaining data integrity, it's important to understand what it entails. Data integrity in Microsoft Forms can be compromised in several ways:

1. Data Entry Errors: Mistakes made during the input of data by respondents or errors in form setup can lead to incorrect data being collected.

2. Data Loss: Accidental deletion of forms, responses, or corrupted files can result in data loss.

3. Data Tampering: Unauthorized access to form responses could lead to intentional or unintentional alteration of data.

4. Inconsistent Data: When multiple versions of a form exist, or when data is exported and manipulated in external applications like Excel, inconsistencies can arise.

5. Technical Glitches: Software bugs, server outages, or sync issues can lead to partial data collection or loss.

To mitigate these risks and ensure that the data collected through Microsoft Forms is reliable and accurate, several best practices can be implemented.

Best Practices for Maintaining Data Integrity in Microsoft Forms

1. Designing Forms with Accuracy in Mind

The foundation of data integrity starts with the form design. A well-designed form minimizes the chances of data entry errors and ensures that the data collected is relevant and accurate.

- Use Field Validation: Microsoft Forms allows you to set specific criteria for responses, such as requiring a certain format for email addresses or numbers. Implementing these validations ensures that the data entered by respondents is in the correct format.

- Mandatory Fields: Make essential fields mandatory to avoid missing critical information. This is particularly important for fields that are key to your data analysis.

- Clear Instructions: Provide clear and concise instructions for each question. This reduces ambiguity and ensures that respondents understand what is required, leading to more accurate responses.

- Logical Flow: Arrange questions in a logical order and use branching logic to guide respondents through the form. This helps in collecting relevant data and reduces the chances of incorrect or irrelevant data being submitted.

2. Regularly Reviewing and Updating Forms

As business needs evolve, the forms you use may need to be updated to reflect new requirements or changes in data collection strategies. Regularly reviewing and updating your forms helps maintain data integrity by ensuring that the forms remain relevant and accurate.

- Scheduled Reviews: Set a regular schedule for reviewing your forms, such as quarterly or annually, depending on the frequency of use and the importance of the data collected.

- Feedback Loop: Use feedback from respondents or form administrators to identify potential issues with the form's design or content that could lead to data inaccuracies.

- Version Control: When updating a form, consider creating a new version rather than modifying the existing one. This allows you to track changes over time and ensures that you can revert to a previous version if needed.

3. Secure Data Handling and Access Control

Data integrity is closely tied to how securely the data is handled and who has access to it. Unauthorized access or mishandling of data can compromise its integrity.

- Access Permissions: Use Microsoft Forms' permissions settings to control who can view, edit, or delete form responses. Limit access to sensitive data to only those who need it.

- Data Encryption: Ensure that data is encrypted both in transit and at rest. While Microsoft Forms automatically encrypts data, understanding and adhering to your organization's data security policies is crucial.

- Audit Trails: Use audit logs and activity tracking features to monitor who accesses or edits form responses. This helps in identifying any unauthorized changes and maintaining the integrity of the data.

4. Data Backup and Recovery

Backing up your data is an essential step in maintaining data integrity. In the event of data loss or corruption, having a backup allows you to restore the original data without significant loss.

- Regular Exports: Export form responses regularly to Excel or another data management tool. This provides an additional layer of security and allows you to analyze data outside of Microsoft Forms.

- Version Backups: If you regularly update your forms, keep backups of previous versions, including the associated data. This ensures that you can restore to a previous state if an update leads to data inconsistencies.

- Disaster Recovery Plan: Develop and implement a disaster recovery plan that includes steps for data recovery in case of accidental deletion, corruption, or other data loss scenarios.

5. Data Quality Checks and Validation

Regular data quality checks help ensure that the data collected remains consistent and accurate over time.

- Automated Checks: Use automated tools or scripts to regularly check for anomalies in your data, such as duplicate entries, missing fields, or outliers that may indicate data entry errors.

- Manual Review: Periodically, manually review a sample of the data to check for consistency and accuracy. This is especially important for critical data that is used in decision-making or compliance reporting.

- Cross-Referencing Data: If your form data is being integrated with other systems (such as CRM or ERP), cross-reference the data with these systems to ensure consistency across platforms.

6. Training and Awareness

Ensuring that everyone involved in the creation, management, and analysis of Microsoft Forms understands the importance of data integrity is key to maintaining high standards.

- Training Sessions: Provide training sessions for form creators and administrators on best practices for data collection, form design, and data management in Microsoft Forms.

- Awareness Campaigns: Conduct awareness campaigns within your organization to emphasize the importance of data integrity and the role that each individual plays in maintaining it.

- Documentation: Maintain detailed documentation on how forms are to be created, managed, and updated, including guidelines on data integrity practices.

7. Utilizing Microsoft 365 Compliance Tools

If your organization uses Microsoft 365, take advantage of the built-in compliance tools to enhance data integrity.

- Data Loss Prevention (DLP): Implement DLP policies to prevent sensitive information from being shared or accessed inappropriately. This is particularly useful if your forms collect confidential or sensitive data.

- eDiscovery and Content Search: Use Microsoft 365's eDiscovery tools to search and manage data across your organization. This helps in identifying any integrity issues and ensuring that data is being managed according to policy.

- Compliance Manager: Use Compliance Manager to assess and manage compliance risks related to data integrity. It provides insights into how data is being handled and whether it adheres to regulatory requirements.

Challenges in Maintaining Data Integrity

Despite the best practices outlined above, maintaining data integrity can present challenges, especially in large organizations or when dealing with complex data sets.

- Scalability: As the volume of data grows, maintaining its integrity becomes more challenging. Automated tools and regular audits become increasingly important in large-scale data collection efforts.

- Human Error: No matter how well-designed a form is, human error in data entry or management can still occur. Continuous training and the use of validation tools can help minimize these errors.

- Integration Issues: When integrating Microsoft Forms with other systems, ensuring data consistency and integrity across platforms can be complex. Regular cross-referencing and the use of integration tools like Power Automate can help mitigate these issues.

- Compliance with Regulations: Adhering to regulations such as GDPR or HIPAA adds an additional layer of complexity to maintaining data integrity. Ensuring that your data handling processes meet regulatory requirements is essential to avoid legal repercussions.

Conclusion

Maintaining data integrity in Microsoft Forms is essential for ensuring that the data you collect is accurate, reliable, and usable for decision-making. By following best practices in form design, data handling, access control, and regular reviews, you can significantly reduce the risks associated with data integrity. Additionally, leveraging the tools available in Microsoft 365 and conducting regular training and awareness campaigns will help create a culture of data integrity within your organization.

Remember, the integrity of your data is not just about protecting it from external threats but also about ensuring that it remains consistent and accurate throughout its lifecycle. By implementing the strategies outlined in this section, you can help ensure that your Microsoft Forms data remains a valuable and reliable resource for your organization.

Appendices

Appendix A: Keyboard Shortcuts for Microsoft Forms

Introduction

Keyboard shortcuts are an essential part of working efficiently with any software, and Microsoft Forms is no exception. Whether you're creating a new survey, managing responses, or customizing settings, knowing the right shortcuts can save time and make your workflow more seamless. This appendix provides a comprehensive guide to keyboard shortcuts available in Microsoft Forms, organized by functionality.

1. General Navigation Shortcuts

These shortcuts allow you to quickly navigate the Microsoft Forms interface without needing to rely on the mouse.

- Tab: Move focus forward through interactive elements (buttons, fields, etc.).

- Shift + Tab: Move focus backward through interactive elements.

- Enter: Select the currently focused item or activate a selected command.

- Esc: Close a dialog box, drop-down menu, or cancel an action.

- Alt + Left Arrow: Go back to the previous page in your browser.

- Alt + Right Arrow: Go forward to the next page in your browser.

Usage Example: When you're navigating through the form creation process, you can use `Tab` to move from the question field to the add question button, and then press `Enter` to select it.

2. Form Creation and Editing Shortcuts

When creating or editing forms, these shortcuts help streamline the process:

- Ctrl + N: Create a new form.

- Ctrl + S: Save the form you're working on.

- Ctrl + Z: Undo the last action.

- Ctrl + Y: Redo the last undone action.

- Ctrl + X: Cut the selected content.

- Ctrl + C: Copy the selected content.

- Ctrl + V: Paste the content from the clipboard.

- Ctrl + A: Select all text or elements in the current field.

- Delete: Remove the selected question or content block.

- F2: Rename a selected element (question title, section name, etc.).

Usage Example: While editing a form, you might decide to copy a question and paste it elsewhere in the form. You can do this quickly with `Ctrl + C` and `Ctrl + V`.

3. Question Types and Formatting Shortcuts

These shortcuts make it easier to format questions and choose specific question types without using the mouse:

- Alt + Q: Add a multiple-choice question.

- Alt + T: Add a text question.

- Alt + R: Add a rating question.

- Alt + D: Add a date question.

- Alt + L: Add a Likert scale question.

- Alt + F: Add a Net Promoter Score (NPS) question.

- Ctrl + B: Bold selected text in the question or answer options.

- Ctrl + I: Italicize selected text.

- Ctrl + U: Underline selected text.

Usage Example: If you're building a form and need to insert a rating question, simply press `Alt + R` to insert it directly into the form.

4. Form Customization Shortcuts

Once your questions are in place, you can use these shortcuts to customize the look and behavior of your form:

- Ctrl + M: Open the theme selector to change the appearance of your form.

- Ctrl + Shift + T: Toggle between different themes.

- Ctrl + Shift + L: Apply branching logic to the selected question.

- Alt + E: Enable or disable required fields for the selected question.

Usage Example: After designing your form, you may want to make certain questions mandatory. You can select each question and press `Alt + E` to toggle the required field setting.

5. Response Management Shortcuts

Managing responses efficiently is crucial, especially when handling large datasets. These shortcuts will help you navigate and manage responses more effectively:

- Ctrl + Shift + V: View the response summary.

- Ctrl + Shift + I: View individual responses.

- Ctrl + Shift + E: Export responses to Excel.

- Ctrl + P: Print responses or summary reports.

- Ctrl + F: Search within responses for specific text or data.

Usage Example: To quickly export all responses to Excel, you can use `Ctrl + Shift + E`, which will open the export options without needing to navigate through the menus.

6. Accessibility Shortcuts

For users who rely on screen readers or other assistive technologies, these shortcuts ensure that Microsoft Forms remains accessible:

- Alt + Shift + S: Open the Accessibility Checker.

- Alt + Shift + D: Describe the selected element (useful for screen readers).

- Ctrl + Alt + Space: Toggle the screen reader on or off.

- Ctrl + Alt + Arrow Keys: Navigate through the form in screen reader mode.

Usage Example: If you need to check whether your form meets accessibility standards, you can press `Alt + Shift + S` to run the Accessibility Checker.

7. Shortcuts for Collaboration and Sharing

Collaborating on a form with others is a key feature of Microsoft Forms. These shortcuts make it easier to manage sharing and collaboration settings:

- Ctrl + Shift + C: Open the collaboration options.

- Ctrl + Shift + U: Open the sharing options to generate a link or QR code.

- Ctrl + Shift + S: Share the form directly via email.

- Ctrl + Shift + M: Manage permissions for collaborators.

Usage Example: When you're ready to share your form with a team member for editing, you can quickly open the collaboration options with `Ctrl + Shift + C`.

8. Shortcuts for Quiz Creation

Quizzes in Microsoft Forms have specific functionalities, such as assigning points and providing feedback. These shortcuts are particularly useful when creating quizzes:

- Ctrl + Shift + Q: Create a new quiz.

- Ctrl + Shift + P: Assign points to the selected question.

- Ctrl + Shift + F: Add feedback for a specific answer.

- Alt + P: Preview the quiz as a respondent would see it.

Usage Example: After setting up a quiz, you might want to preview it to ensure everything looks correct. Press `Alt + P` to view the quiz as it will appear to respondents.

9. Shortcuts for Microsoft Teams Integration

Microsoft Forms integrates seamlessly with Microsoft Teams, and these shortcuts help manage forms within Teams:

- Ctrl + Shift + G: Create a new form directly in a Teams channel.

- Ctrl + Shift + R: Review form responses within Teams.

- Alt + G: Share a form with a Teams channel or individual.

- Ctrl + Shift + N: Notify a Teams channel about a new form or quiz.

Usage Example: To quickly create a form within a Teams channel, use `Ctrl + Shift + G` to initiate the form creation process without leaving Teams.

10. Customizing and Managing Settings

Beyond just creating and editing forms, managing overall settings is also important. These shortcuts make it easier to access and modify settings:

- Alt + O: Open form settings to manage things like who can fill out the form, start and end dates, and notifications.

- Ctrl + Shift + A: Access advanced settings for more customization options.

- Ctrl + Shift + P: Preview settings to see how changes will affect the form.

- Ctrl + Shift + H: Toggle between hiding and showing the toolbar.

Usage Example: When fine-tuning who can respond to your form, press `Alt + O` to open the form settings directly and adjust permissions or response options.

11. Miscellaneous Shortcuts

These shortcuts don't fit neatly into other categories but are still useful for a smoother experience:

- F1: Open the help menu for Microsoft Forms.

- Ctrl + ?: Open a list of all available keyboard shortcuts within Microsoft Forms.

- Ctrl + Shift + L: Open the list of all forms you've created or have access to.

- Alt + 1, 2, 3...: Quickly switch between different forms (useful if you have multiple forms open at once).

Usage Example: If you're ever unsure about which shortcut to use, pressing `Ctrl + ?` will display a list of all the shortcuts available to you, helping you learn and apply them more easily.

Conclusion

Mastering keyboard shortcuts for Microsoft Forms can greatly enhance your efficiency and streamline your workflow. Whether you're creating a simple survey, designing an in-depth quiz, or managing responses, these shortcuts allow you to perform tasks quickly without constantly reaching for the mouse. By integrating these shortcuts into your daily routine, you'll find yourself navigating and managing Microsoft Forms with greater ease, allowing more focus on content creation and data analysis rather than the mechanics of the interface.

This appendix has covered a broad range of shortcuts, from basic navigation to advanced form management. As you continue using Microsoft Forms, you'll likely discover which shortcuts are most valuable for your specific workflow. Keep this guide handy as a quick reference, and don't hesitate to explore and experiment with these shortcuts to maximize your productivity.

Appendix B: Glossary of Terms

In this glossary, you'll find definitions and explanations of key terms and concepts that are essential for understanding and using Microsoft Forms effectively. This section is designed to serve as a quick reference guide for both beginners and advanced users.

1. Accessibility

Refers to the practice of making Microsoft Forms usable by people of all abilities and disabilities. Accessibility features ensure that all users, including those with disabilities, can interact with and complete forms or quizzes without difficulty.

2. Analytics

The process of collecting, analyzing, and interpreting data from form responses. Microsoft Forms provides built-in analytics tools that allow users to view response summaries, trends, and individual responses in a visual format.

3. Anonymous Responses

A setting in Microsoft Forms that allows respondents to submit their answers without revealing their identity. This is useful for collecting honest feedback without influencing respondents' answers due to privacy concerns.

4. Auto-save

A feature in Microsoft Forms that automatically saves changes to your form or quiz as you work. This ensures that no progress is lost in case of accidental closure or other interruptions.

5. Branching Logic

A functionality in Microsoft Forms that allows the creator to set up conditional logic, where subsequent questions are shown or hidden based on the respondent's previous answers. This makes the form more dynamic and personalized.

6. Collaboration

The process of working together with others to create, edit, or manage a form. Microsoft Forms allows multiple users to collaborate on a single form or quiz in real-time, facilitating teamwork and shared responsibility.

7. Conditional Formatting

A feature that allows users to apply formatting changes to a form or its data based on specific criteria. In the context of Microsoft Forms, this might involve highlighting certain answers or adjusting the appearance of a form element based on responses.

8. Data Export

The process of exporting form response data from Microsoft Forms to other applications, such as Excel. This allows users to perform more detailed analysis, create reports, or share data with others.

9. Distribution

Refers to the methods used to share a form or quiz with respondents. Microsoft Forms provides several distribution options, including sharing via a link, email, QR code, or embedding the form in a webpage.

10. Dropdown Question

A type of question in Microsoft Forms that presents respondents with a list of options in a dropdown menu. This format is useful for questions where space is limited or when there are many possible answers.

11. Embedding

The process of integrating a Microsoft Form into a webpage, email, or another digital platform. Embedding allows users to access and complete the form without navigating away from the current page.

12. Feedback

Information provided to respondents after they submit their answers. In Microsoft Forms, feedback can be customized for each question, providing explanations or additional information based on the respondent's answers.

13. Likert Scale

A type of question that allows respondents to indicate their level of agreement or disagreement with a statement on a scale (e.g., Strongly Agree to Strongly Disagree). Likert scales are commonly used in surveys to measure attitudes and opinions.

14. Multiple Choice Question

A question type in Microsoft Forms where respondents are given a list of possible answers and must select one or more. Multiple choice questions are versatile and can be used for a wide range of survey or quiz scenarios.

15. Net Promoter Score (NPS)

A metric used to gauge customer loyalty by asking respondents how likely they are to recommend a product or service to others. In Microsoft Forms, an NPS question typically uses a scale from 0 to 10 and categorizes respondents as promoters, passives, or detractors.

16. Preview Mode

A feature in Microsoft Forms that allows the form creator to view the form as respondents will see it. This mode is used to test the form's appearance and functionality before distribution.

17. Quiz

A type of form in Microsoft Forms specifically designed for assessments, tests, or knowledge checks. Quizzes allow for scoring, automatic feedback, and the tracking of respondent performance.

18. Ranking Question

A type of question that asks respondents to order items according to their preference or priority. Ranking questions are useful for understanding relative importance or preference among options.

19. Real-time Collaboration

The ability for multiple users to work on a form simultaneously. Microsoft Forms supports real-time collaboration, allowing changes to be seen and edited by all collaborators as they happen.

20. Response Rate

The percentage of people who respond to a form or survey out of those who received it. A higher response rate generally indicates greater engagement or interest in the survey topic.

21. Response Summary

A visual representation of the overall results from a form or quiz. Microsoft Forms automatically generates a response summary that includes charts, graphs, and key metrics for easy analysis.

22. Required Question

A setting in Microsoft Forms that makes a question mandatory, meaning respondents cannot submit the form without answering it. Required questions are used to ensure that critical data is collected.

23. Scoring

The process of assigning points to quiz answers in Microsoft Forms. Scoring is used to evaluate respondent performance and can be automated, with results provided immediately after submission.

24. Section

A feature that allows form creators to organize questions into different groups or sections. Sections can be used to logically separate different topics or stages within a form, making it easier for respondents to navigate.

25. Share Options

The various methods provided by Microsoft Forms to share forms and quizzes with others. Share options include generating a shareable link, sending via email, or embedding the form on a website.

26. Short Answer Question

A type of question that allows respondents to provide brief, open-ended responses. Short answer questions are typically used for qualitative data or when respondents need to provide a specific piece of information.

27. Survey

A form in Microsoft Forms used to collect information, opinions, or feedback from respondents. Surveys can include a variety of question types and are often used for research, customer feedback, or employee engagement.

28. Text Question

A type of question that allows respondents to enter freeform text responses. Text questions are useful for gathering open-ended feedback or detailed explanations from respondents.

29. Themes

Pre-designed color schemes and styles that can be applied to a form to enhance its appearance. Microsoft Forms offers a variety of themes, allowing users to customize the look and feel of their forms.

30. Timestamp

The recorded date and time when a respondent submits a form or quiz. Timestamps are useful for tracking when responses were collected and for time-sensitive data analysis.

31. Validation

Rules that can be applied to form fields to ensure that the data entered by respondents meets certain criteria. For example, you can validate that an email address field contains a properly formatted email address.

32. Version History

A record of changes made to a form over time. Version history allows form creators to view previous versions of a form, track edits, and revert to an earlier version if necessary.

33. Video Question

A question type in Microsoft Forms that allows the inclusion of a video for respondents to watch before answering a related question. This is useful for quizzes or educational forms where context or instruction is needed.

34. Weighted Scoring

A method of assigning different point values to different answers within a quiz. Weighted scoring allows for more nuanced assessments of respondent knowledge or performance.

35. Workflow Integration

The process of integrating Microsoft Forms with other tools and systems to automate workflows. This might involve sending form data to a database, triggering notifications, or updating records in another application.

36. Yes/No Question

A simple binary question format where respondents choose between two options, typically "Yes" or "No." Yes/No questions are commonly used for clear, straightforward inquiries.

37. QR Code

A scannable code that can be generated by Microsoft Forms to allow respondents to access the form via their mobile devices. QR codes are an easy way to distribute forms in physical settings, such as events or classrooms.

38. Respondent

The individual who answers or completes a form or quiz. Understanding respondent behavior and demographics is critical for analyzing form data effectively.

39. Microsoft 365

A subscription service from Microsoft that includes access to Microsoft Forms along with other productivity tools like Word, Excel, PowerPoint, and Teams. Microsoft Forms is often used in conjunction with these other tools.

40. Poll

A quick survey typically consisting of a single question or a few questions used to gauge opinions or preferences. Polls are often used in meetings or presentations to engage participants.

41. Form Template

A pre-designed form that can be used as a starting point for creating a new form. Templates help save time and ensure consistency across similar forms.

42. Insights

Data-driven conclusions and observations drawn from analyzing form responses. Insights can guide decision-making, improve processes, and provide valuable feedback.

43. Logic Jump

A type of conditional logic in Microsoft Forms that allows respondents to skip certain sections of a form based on their answers. This feature helps to create a more streamlined and relevant experience for the respondent.

44. SharePoint

A web-based collaboration platform that integrates with Microsoft Forms. SharePoint can be used to store and manage form data, as well as to collaborate on form creation within an organization.

45. Embedding

The integration of a Microsoft Form into a webpage, blog post, or email. Embedding allows respondents to complete forms directly from the embedded location without being redirected.

46. Forms Pro

An enhanced version of Microsoft Forms,

providing additional features such as advanced analytics, customization options, and integration capabilities. Forms Pro is often used for enterprise-level surveys and customer feedback.

47. Response Time

The amount of time it takes a respondent to complete a form or quiz. Understanding response times can help improve form design and identify areas where respondents may struggle.

48. Survey Logic

Conditional rules applied to a survey to control which questions are displayed based on previous answers. Survey logic is used to create a more tailored experience and to ensure that respondents only see relevant questions.

49. Data Privacy

The protection of personal data collected through forms and surveys. Microsoft Forms includes features to help ensure that data is stored securely and that respondents' privacy is respected.

50. Engagement

The level of interaction and involvement that respondents have with a form or survey. High engagement typically leads to more accurate and useful data, while low engagement may result in incomplete or unreliable responses.

Conclusion

Recap of Key Concepts

As we reach the conclusion of "Microsoft Forms: Complete Guide for Effective Surveys and Quizzes," it is essential to reflect on the journey we've undertaken together throughout this book. From understanding the basics of Microsoft Forms to mastering its advanced features, we've explored the full potential of this powerful tool.

We began by laying the groundwork with a thorough introduction to Microsoft Forms, discussing its purpose and the various scenarios in which it can be employed effectively. Whether you are an educator looking to create interactive quizzes, a business professional needing to gather feedback, or an individual interested in organizing surveys, Microsoft Forms provides a versatile platform that caters to a wide array of needs.

The subsequent chapters walked you through the detailed process of creating your first form. You learned how to design engaging and functional surveys by selecting the right templates, customizing layouts, and incorporating various question types. The importance of thoughtful design cannot be overstated; a well-crafted form not only gathers the required data but also enhances the user experience, leading to higher response rates and more accurate results.

As you delved deeper into the book, you gained insights into customizing your forms to make them more effective. We discussed how to apply themes, utilize branching logic, and add media elements like images and videos to make your forms more interactive and visually appealing. Accessibility features were also highlighted, ensuring that your forms are inclusive and usable by a diverse audience.

In managing form responses, you discovered the importance of collecting and analyzing data efficiently. The tools within Microsoft Forms allow you to view response summaries, analyze individual responses, and export data for further analysis in applications like Excel. This ability to transform raw data into actionable insights is one of the core strengths of Microsoft Forms.

For those looking to create quizzes, the book provided a comprehensive guide to setting up and managing quizzes within Microsoft Forms. From choosing appropriate question types to setting up scoring and feedback mechanisms, you've learned how to create quizzes that are not only educational but also engaging for participants.

The advanced features and integrations chapter showcased the flexibility of Microsoft Forms, demonstrating how it integrates seamlessly with other Microsoft 365 applications and third-party tools. Whether you are using Forms within Microsoft Teams or linking it with SharePoint, these integrations help streamline your workflows and maximize the efficiency of your operations.

Finally, the best practices chapter offered practical advice on designing effective forms and quizzes. From writing clear and concise questions to strategies for increasing response rates and ensuring data privacy, these tips are invaluable for anyone looking to create impactful forms.

Reflection on the Power of Microsoft Forms

The true power of Microsoft Forms lies in its simplicity coupled with its depth of functionality. It's a tool that democratizes data collection, making it accessible to anyone regardless of their technical background. This book has shown you how to harness that power, providing you with the knowledge and skills to create forms and quizzes that are not only functional but also impactful.

As you continue to use Microsoft Forms in your personal or professional life, remember that the key to success is not just in the tool itself, but in how you use it. Effective forms and quizzes require careful planning, thoughtful design, and ongoing refinement based on feedback and results. With the knowledge you've gained from this book, you are well-equipped to create forms that serve your specific needs while delivering valuable insights.

Encouragement for Continued Learning

While this book has covered a broad range of topics, Microsoft Forms is a tool that continues to evolve. New features and integrations are regularly added, and staying updated with these changes will further enhance your ability to create effective forms and quizzes. I encourage you to continue exploring Microsoft Forms beyond the content of this book. Experiment with different features, seek out additional resources, and engage with the online community to learn from others' experiences.

Remember, the best way to master a tool is through practice. The more you use Microsoft Forms, the more proficient you will become in creating forms that are both functional and engaging. Keep experimenting, keep learning, and most importantly, keep creating.

Acknowledgments

Gratitude to Readers

I want to extend my deepest gratitude to you, the reader, for choosing this book and embarking on this journey with me. Writing "Microsoft Forms: Complete Guide for Effective Surveys and Quizzes" has been a labor of love, and knowing that this book is in your hands, serving as a resource to help you achieve your goals, is incredibly fulfilling.

Your trust in this book is something I do not take lightly, and I sincerely hope that the knowledge shared here empowers you to use Microsoft Forms to its fullest potential. Whether you're a beginner or an experienced user, I hope you've found value in these pages and that the content has enriched your understanding of Microsoft Forms.

Acknowledgment of Supporters and Contributors

This book would not have been possible without the support and encouragement of many individuals. I would like to take a moment to acknowledge and thank those who contributed to the creation of this book.

First and foremost, I would like to thank my family for their unwavering support throughout this process. Writing a book is a time-consuming endeavor, and their patience and understanding made it possible for me to dedicate the time and energy required to complete this project.

I am also deeply grateful to my editor, whose keen eye and insightful feedback were invaluable in shaping the content of this book. Their dedication to ensuring clarity, accuracy, and coherence in every chapter has significantly improved the final product.

A special thank you goes to the technical reviewers who lent their expertise to this project. Their thorough review of the content ensured that the information presented is not only accurate but also practical and applicable. Their contributions have helped make this book a reliable resource for readers.

I would also like to express my appreciation to the team at the publishing house who worked tirelessly behind the scenes to bring this book to life. From the initial concept to the final publication, their professionalism and expertise have been instrumental in making this book a reality.

Finally, I would like to thank the Microsoft Forms community. The knowledge and experiences shared by users around the world provided valuable insights that enriched the content of this book. The community's willingness to share best practices, tips, and solutions is a testament to the collaborative spirit that drives innovation and learning.

Final Thoughts

As I conclude this book, I want to leave you with a final thought: The journey of learning never truly ends. While this book may mark the end of one chapter, it is also the beginning of your continued exploration of Microsoft Forms and its possibilities. Use this book as a foundation, but don't hesitate to build upon it with your own experiences and discoveries.

Thank you once again for choosing this book. I wish you all the best in your endeavors with Microsoft Forms and hope that this book has provided you with the tools and inspiration to create effective and impactful surveys and quizzes.

Happy form building!